OREGON TRIVIA
Weird, Wacky and Wild

Mark Thorburn & Lisa Wojna
Illustrations by Roger Garcia & Patrick Hénaff

BLUE
BIKE
BOOKS

© 2021 by Blue Bike Books

All rights reserved. No part of this work covered by the copyrights hereon may be reproduced or used in any form or by any means—graphic, electronic or mechanical—without the prior written permission of the publisher, except for reviewers, who may quote brief passages. Any request for photocopying, recording, taping or storage on information retrieval systems of any part of this work shall be directed in writing to the publisher.

The Publisher: Blue Bike Books Ltd.
Website: www.bluebikebooks.com

Library and Archives Canada Cataloguing in Publication
 Title: Oregon trivia : weird, wacky and wild / Mark Thorburn & Lisa Wojna ; illustrations by Roger Garcia & Patrick Hénaff.
Other titles: Bathroom book of Oregon trivia
Names: Thorburn, Mark. author. | Wojna, Lisa, 1962– author. | Garcia, Roger, 1976– illustrator. |
         Hénaff, Patrick, illustrator.
Description: Previously published under title: Bathroom book of Oregon trivia. Edmonton: Blue Bike Books, 2007.
Identifiers: Canadiana 20210332344 | ISBN 9781989209240 (softcover)
Subjects: LCSH: Oregon—Miscellanea.
Classification: LCC F876.6 .T56 2021 | DDC 979.5002—dc23

Project Director: Nicholle Carrière
Project Editor: Brian Crane
Production: Alexander Penrose, Alicia West
Illustrations: Roger Garcia, Patrick Hénaff

Produced with the assistance of the Government of Alberta.

We acknowledge the financial support of the Government of Canada.
Nous reconnaissons l'appui financier du gouvernement du Canada..

PC: 40

DEDICATION

To my niece, Kate

–Mark

ACKNOWLEDGMENTS

Many thanks to Blue Bike Books for the opportunity to work on this project. And thank you also to my editor, Brian Crane, and to my co-author, Lisa Wojna, for their wonderful skills, tremendous insights, and marvelous contributions—hey guys, we make a great team!

–Mark

Many thanks to my clever editor, Brian, who pieced together the work of two authors and did so seamlessly, to my co-author Mark and to my family—my husband Garry, sons Peter, Matthew and Nathan, daughter Melissa and granddaughter Jada. Without you, all this and anything else I do in my life would be meaningless.

–Lisa

CONTENTS

INTRODUCTION 6
NAMES AND SYMBOLS
The Naming of a State 8
State Symbols 10
They Oughta Be State Symbols 16
CLIMATE AND WEATHER
Averages and Extremes 17
Deadly Disasters 19
GEOGRAPHIC GENERALITIES
General Geography 22
Oregon's Coastline, Lakes and Rivers 25
Volcanoes 33
Glaciers, Mountains and Whatnot 38
ENVIRONMENT
Forest Lands 43
Conservation and Parklands 48
Our Flying Friends 50
POPULATION
By The Numbers 52
Native Americans 63
French Canadians 65
TOURISM AND TRIVIA
Roadside Attractions 67
Lighthouses 71
Natural Attractions 74
Architectural Attractions 77
MUSEUMS AND FESTIVALS
Museums 79
Fun in the Sun 85
Ye Olde Faires! 92
Music Festivals 94
PORTLAND
The City of Roses 95
Eat, Drink and Be Merry 104
Portland Parks 108
CITY TRIVIA
Facts and Figures 110
Fun City Facts 113

COUNTY TRIVIA
Just the Facts!. 119
Claims to Fame 122
Counties Named After Famous Folks 124

NAMES AND PLACES
City Names 129
Places that Remind People of Home 134
Mysterious Names 136
Name Changes 138

HISTORIC HAPPENINGS
Firsts, Oldests, Etc. 140
Ghost Towns 147
Founding Mothers and Fathers 153
Traveling the Oregon Trail 156

ECONOMY
The Basics 160
Agriculture, Forestry and Fishing 163
By the Numbers 165
Oregon's Businesses Mean Business! 170

CULINARY ADVENTURES
Tempting the Taste Buds 175

EDUCATION
Higher Education 178
Elementary and Secondary Education 187
Higher Ed Quick Facts 194

POLITICS
Presidential Politics 196
Blue vs. Red 199

TRANSPORTATION
Highways and Driving Habits 203

CELEBRITIES
Hollywood in Oregon 206
The Press and Pulitzers 208
Some Notable Oregonians 210

OREGON SPORTS
Sports Heroes 213
Outdoor Fun 215

SCIENCE AND TECHNOLOGY
Inventions and Gadgets 217
Nobel Prize Winners 219

A FEW LAST WORDS
Top Ten Reasons to Live in Oregon 222

INTRODUCTION

Oregon is unique.

It spans from a coastal mountain range and valley that's often so wet that people make jokes about the rain to a moonlike desert where NASA practiced lunar walks. The state includes massive rivers, deep blue lakes, giant forests, sand dunes, alpine mountains and some of the most beautiful scenery in the world.

One of the hardest hit by the recession of the early 2000s, Oregon is now one of the fastest growing states in the country.

Politically, the Beaver State is just as divided between "blue" and "red" as the rest of the country, but it is still known for leading the way in such progressive ideas as a high minimum wage, voting by mail, environmental protection and the Oregon Health Plan.

Oregon is home to a diverse group of folks that includes cowboys and hippies, devout believers and atheists, people whose families have been in the state for generations and recent immigrants who have come from over 100 countries.

And our state is special in countless other ways. Volumes would be needed to list them all, but what better way to begin than with a trivia book?

Trivia is a quick, entertaining, sometimes humorous and always educational introduction to any topic, and there is an enormous supply of little-known facts and statistics, eccentricities and tidbits, and great stories and anecdotes about the state of Oregon. Who won't chuckle when they learn that Oregon has the largest hairball and the smallest restaurant in the world as well as a doughnut shop that performs weddings between Swahili lessons and a park that was originally intended for the enjoyment of the little folk of Ireland?

What Oregonian is not proud to learn that the state boasts some of the best colleges and universities in the United States and that, as our high school drop out rate has gone down, the number of graduates who have gone on to college has gone up? Who would not be interested to know that Oregon has been home to some of the greatest entertainers and scientists of our time; is the place where many national and multinational businesses have begun; and has the best, the most, the first and the only of so many wonderful things? And what person does not enjoy sitting around the kitchen or the cocktail bar shooting the breeze and trying to outdo their family and friends with little scraps of knowledge?

If anything, the trouble is that there is so much wonderful trivia out there! Fortunately, behind every trivia book, there is an editor and a publisher who reins things in.

Here is a selection of facts and statistics that we have dug up for your entertainment. Hopefully, you will enjoy them and learn as much by reading them as we had in discovering, researching and writing about them.

NAMES AND SYMBOLS

THE NAMING OF A STATE

Log on to your favorite search engine, look up the history of the name "Oregon," and you'll quickly discover several different theories about its origin. Some possibilities?

- The French-Canadian word *ourang*, which means "storm" or "hurricane" and refers to the ferocious Columbia River

- The Spanish word *orejon*, a nickname meaning "big ear" given to some Native American tribes

NAMES AND SYMBOLS

- The Spanish word oregano, as in the wild herb that is quite prolific in the eastern portion of the state
- The Native American name for the Columbia River, "the great Ouragon"
- The Native American word oolighan, which means "fish grease," an item often traded between early settlers and indigenous peoples

The first recorded use of the name Oregon is Major Robert Roger's 1765 call for an expedition "to the River called by the Indians Ouragon." The name was used again in Jonathan Carver's 1778 book *Travels Through the Interior Parts of North America: 1766, 1767 and 1768.*

In 1793, future President Thomas Jefferson used the name to refer to a river. And in 1821 poet William Cullen Bryant referred to Oregon in his poem, *Thanatopsis.* The territory was officially named Oregon on January 18, 1822.

DID YOU  KNOW?

Back in the 1700s, there was a little confusion as to where Oregon was exactly. On some early maps, Wisconsin bore the name! The mistake seems to have happened because the Wisconsin River was known originally as the Ouisconsink River. This was misspelled as "Ouracon" and the mapmakers of the day changed it even further to Oregon.

ନAMES AND SYMBOLS

STATE SYMBOLS

Motto

Oregon's state motto—*Alis volat Proprilis*—means "She flies with her own wings." Judge Jessie Quinn Thornton coined the phrase, and it was translated into Latin for the territorial seal in 1854.

The motto was said to reflect the independence of the Oregon pioneers who established their own provisional government in 1843 rather than remain under the wings of Britain or the United States.

In 1957, the motto was changed to "The Union," a reference to historic conflicts over slavery, but in 1987, the legislature re-adopted the original motto.

Famous birthday
In Oregon, February 14 isn't just for sweethearts. It's also Oregon's birthday! Oregon joined the Union on February 14, 1859, making it the 33rd state of the United States.

Otherwise known as
Oregon's nickname is the Beaver State. It's also been known as the Sunset State and the Union State.

State Flag

With a different image on each side, the flag adopted by Oregon in 1925 is definitely one of a kind. On the front, the state seal is woven in gold on a field of blue. Above the seal is written "State of Oregon" and beneath it "1859." On the back is an image of a beaver.

What a Gem!

The Oregon sunstone was chosen as the official state gemstone in 1987. The stone is a type of Labradorite, which is a kind of feldspar that bends light in three different directions. Known to geologists as heliolite and as plagioclase feldspar, the Oregon sunstone is famous for its uncommon clarity and its wide range of bright colors. They've been found in every color but purple!

The stones vary in size from small flakes to chunks as big as your thumb. They can only be found near Plush, and are sometimes called Plush diamonds. In the "olden days," you could find them lying on the ground, but most sunstones are now recovered in open-pit mines. The Bureau of Land Management has established a four-square-mile, "free-use" collecting area for the general public. The stones are extremely popular and can be found in many gift shops and jewelry stores…but they're expensive!

Once cleaned and cut, a sunstone's is brighter than the sun's reflection in a mirror. In fact, the mysterious morning lights that explorer Charles Fremont and his men saw in the distance when they visited southern Oregon may have been sunlight reflecting on sunstones. Local Native Americans once used the gems as a form of currency.

State Animals

The Chinook salmon, the largest Pacific salmon, has been Oregon's state fish since 1961. Also known as spring salmon, king salmon, tyee salmon and Columbia River salmon, they are found from southern California to the Arctic.

The Oregon swallowtail butterfly is the state insect. Adopted as a state symbol in 1979, it has beautiful yellow wings with concave spots as well as a yellow abdomen with black lines. Found only in the Pacific Northwest, it lives in the lower canyons of the Columbia River and its tributaries.

Oregon declared the American beaver the state animal in 1969. The beaver was hunted throughout Oregon and the Pacific Northwest by the Hudson's Bay Company's trappers in the early 19th century.

To help choose the state bird, the Audubon Society polled Oregon's school children in 1927. The kids picked the western meadowlark. Found throughout western North America, it is brown with a bright yellow underside. It has a black crescent on its chest and white tail feathers. The western meadowlark also sings a pretty tune.

Other Symbols and Emblems

The Douglas fir was declared Oregon's official tree in 1939. Also known as the Oregon pine, it is found along the coast and on the west side of the Cascade Mountains. The trees reach an average height of 200 feet, but can grow as high as 325 feet. Its wood is stronger than concrete!

Oregon's state flower is the Oregon grape, adopted in 1899. This unique plant is not a grape, but a shrub. It is native to the Pacific Coast from British Columbia to northern California and has holly-like leaves, yellow flowers and tart, purple fruit that is often used to make jelly.

The Oregon hairy triton was declared the state's official seashell in 1989. Found on the coast from Alaska to California and on the coast of northern Japan, these beautiful shells wash up on the Oregon coast at high tide.

"Oregon, My Oregon," written by J.A. Buchanan of Astoria and composed by Henry B. Murtagh of Portland, was designated the state song in 1927 after a Society of Oregon Composers' competition.

The Portland Trail Blazers were declared Oregon's official state team in 1991.

Milk became Oregon's official state beverage in 1997.

Navy blue and gold were declared Oregon's official state colors in 1959.

The square dance was designated Oregon's official state dance in 1977.

Every year since 1969, Miss Oregon has served as the state's official hostess. In 2002, Katie Harman of Gresham became the first Miss Oregon to win the Miss America title.

OREGON'S AWESOME! Oregon's state fruit is the pear. The state produces four varieties: Comice, Anjou, Bosc and Bartlett. There are nearly 400 pear growers in Oregon and over 19,000 acres are devoted to the crop. Nearly 800 million pears are grown every year in the state, and Oregon ranks second among the fresh pear-producing states in the country!

Other State Foods

The hazelnut has been Oregon's official nut since 1989. Ninety-nine percent of the entire American crop is grown in the state and the unique texture and flavor of Oregon's hazelnut makes it an item desired by cooks and connoisseurs around the world.

The flower-shaped Pacific golden chanterelle is Oregon's state mushroom. This edible, yellow-orange mushroom with a fruity fragrance and chewy texture is found only in the Pacific Northwest. More than a half million pounds of the famed fungus are harvested in Oregon every year. It was declared Oregon's official mushroom in 1999.

When a Rock is Not a Rock

The thunderegg was declared Oregon's official state rock in 1965…but it's not a rock at all! It's a geode. Formed in volcanic ash beds, these plain, nondescript lumps don't look like much from the outside. But break them open, and you'll find beautiful agate, jasper and opal crystals. Thundereggs range in size from one inch to over four feet in diameter and can be found in central and southeastern Oregon.

NAMES AND SYMBOLS

Oregon's Newest Symbol

You might say that the state's newest symbol is a living fossil! *Metasequoia* trees once covered central and eastern Oregon, but hadn't been seen anywhere except in fossils for five million years. Then in the 1940s, a grove of 100-foot *Metasequoia* was discovered in China, and saplings were brought back to the United States. The tree can now be admired at Willson Park on the state capitol grounds and for sale at local nurseries. It's better known as the dawn redwood and has been an official state symbol since 2005.

THEY OUGHTA BE STATE SYMBOLS!

The Marionberry

The dark purple marionberry was developed at Oregon State University in 1956 as a cross between Chehalem and olallieberry blackberries. Today, over 30 million pounds are grown every year in the Willamette Valley. The berries have a sweet but mildly tart taste and are great fresh, frozen, dried or canned. They also make fantastic wine.

Myrtlewood

What Oregonian is not familiar with the beautiful myrtlewood found only on the coasts of southwest Oregon and northwest California? Its color, which ranges from blond to black with many shades of honey, red and green, depends upon the minerals in the soil, and its grain patterns take many finishes well. Its leaves have a pungent, spicy odor and are used in perfume, incense, scented candles and for cooking.

DID YOU KNOW?

The state's largest myrtlewood tree is 88 feet tall with a canopy nearly 70 feet wide. It's 42 feet in circumference! You can find the tree along the Rogue River about 10 miles east of Gold Beach.

CLIMATE AND WEATHER

AVERAGES AND EXTREMES

Oregon's average high temperature is 82.6°F. The average low is 32.8°F.

Misery Loves Company
Two communities have recorded Oregon's highest temperature. Pendleton hit 119°F on July 29, 1898. Prineville hit the same mark on August 10 of the same year.

Two communities also share Oregon's lowest temperature! Ukiah recorded a chilly –54°F on February 9, 1933. Seneca dropped to the same mark the very next day!

Winter Wonderland?
The most snow to fall in a single day in Oregon was 39 inches, recorded at the Bonneville Dam in January 9, 1980.

Crater Lake recorded 313 inches of snowfall in January 1950. That's the largest one-month accumulation in the state's history. It recorded the largest annual snowfall the same year: 903 inches!

We're having a heat wave

From July 21 to 24, 2006, parts of Oregon experienced a heat wave that ushered in record-breaking temperatures. Portland airport recorded a record high of 104°F on July 21. On July 23, both the Salem and the Eugene airports reported a scorching 105°F. But the highest of the highs was recorded at Medford airport—temperatures there shot up to 106°F on July 22 and to 107°F the next day.

CLIMATE AND WEATHER

Swim with the Fishes

Wettest day? On November 19, 1996, Port Orford recorded 11.65 inches of precipitation.

Wettest month? In December 1917, Glenora recorded 52.78 inches of precipitation!

Wettest year? In 1996, Laurel Mountain recorded 204.12 inches of precipitation.

DID YOU  KNOW?

The driest year in Oregon history was 1939. That year, the Warm Springs Reservoir recorded a paltry 3.33 inches of precipitation!

CLIMATE AND WEATHER

DEADLY DISASTERS

Heppner Floods

When a thunderstorm caused flash flooding along Willow Creek in 1903, a 40-foot wall of water destroyed Heppner and left 247 people dead. One resident, Leslie Matlock, escaped with his life when he rode off on horseback to warn people living in nearby Lexington to head for the hills. Thankfully, the town's 500 residents listened because the flood destroyed all but two of their homes. Twenty miles away at Ione, another 150 homes were destroyed.

Despite producing Oregon's deadliest natural disaster, there are no official records of the storm. The area's weather observation post was destroyed by the flood, killing the observer and his family.

The Vanport Dike
Fifteen people were killed and 10,000 homes destroyed at Vanport in 1946 when the floodwaters of the Columbia River pushed through a 200-foot section of the dike protecting the city. After only two hours, the entire community was 15 feet underwater! Vanport was never rebuilt, but the Portland International Raceway and Delta Park now occupy the site.

Western and Central Oregon Floods
The December 1964 rainstorm was one of the most severe in Oregon's history. Much of central Oregon received two-thirds of its normal annual rainfall in only five days, and 24-hour and December rainfall records were broken all over the state. The subsequent flooding killed 17 people and caused the evacuation of thousands. Hundreds of miles of highway and road were washed away, countless homes and buildings were destroyed or damaged and the newly built John Day Bridge was swept away.

Tillamook Fire

In 1933, a small fire at a logging operation at Gales Creek Canyon in northwest Oregon spread to 40,000 acres in only two days. Ten days later, a quarter million acres were burning.

Smoke from the fire went eight miles into the sky. Ash fell on ships as far as 500 miles at sea and piled up two feet thick along one 30-mile stretch of coastline! The heat a quarter of a mile away from the fire was 120°F. At one point, over 3000 fire-fighters fought the inferno along an 18-mile front!

Mother Nature eventually extinguished the fire with rain. Over 270,000 acres of forest were destroyed at an estimated cost of $200 million. Put another way, as much timber burned in the fire as had been processed in all of the sawmills in the United States in 1932.

Columbus Day Windstorms

In 1962, extremely high winds tore through much of Oregon to disastrous effect. Thirty-eight people were killed, over 50,000 homes were damaged and many cities were without power for two to three weeks. Wind gusts of over 100 miles per hour were recorded at Corvallis, Newport, Portland and Troutdale. Winds of more than 60 miles per hour were clocked at several other locations. Farmers were hit especially hard. Orchards were uprooted, barns blown down and hundreds of animals killed. The total cost of the destruction was between $170 and $200 million.

DID YOU  KNOW?

More trees were leveled by the Columbus Day windstorm—15 times as many, in fact—than by the 1980 eruption of Mount St. Helens.

GEOGRAPHIC GENERALITIES

GENERAL GEOGRAPHY

The Lay of the Land
Oregon borders Washington to the north, Idaho to the east, Nevada and California to the south, and the Pacific Ocean to the west. From east to west, the state measures about 360 miles and from north to south about 261 miles.

Most geographers divide the state into six regions:

- the Coast Range
- the Willamette Lowland
- the Cascade Mountains
- Klamath Mountains
- Columbia River Plateau
- the Basin and Range Region

The variation between Oregon's regions is extreme. For example, the Willamette Valley is considered one of the best agricultural areas of the world, but there are areas in eastern Oregon that receive so little annual rainfall that they qualify as deserts! In the west, a chain of tall volcanoes forms the Cascade Mountains. They are part of the Pacific Ring of Fire and, over 15 million years, their lava flow built up the Columbia River Plateau. The Columbia River Gorge was then cut away by Ice Age glaciers!

Just How Big Is Oregon?

The Oregon Blue Book claims Oregon is 96,002 square miles in size, but the U.S. Census Bureau claims it covers an area of 98,386 square miles. The difference—more than 2000 square miles—is caused by all of Oregon's lakes and rivers: the federal government counts them as part of the surface area, but the state doesn't. The difference matters: Oregon's measurements make it the 10th largest state, but the Census Bureau ranks it ninth! (Sorry about that, Wyoming.)

Publicly Owned Land

The federal government owns almost 57 percent of Oregon's land. Most of it is under the control of the Forest Service and the Bureau of Land Management. The state and local governments own another three percent.

DID YOU KNOW?

The geographic center of Oregon is 25 miles south-southeast of Prineville.

The Highest and The Lowest

Mount Hood is the highest point in Oregon, towering 11,239 feet above sea level. It is an active volcano that rumbles every now and then.

Hells Canyon on the northern Oregon-Idaho border is the deepest river-cut gorge in North America. It's 150 miles long, 10 miles wide and, at He Devil Peak in Idaho, 8043 feet deep. That's a third of a mile deeper than the Grand Canyon! You can see it at the 652,000-acre Hells Canyon National Recreational Area.

DID YOU  KNOW?

Average all the high and low points in Oregon and you'll find a mean elevation of 3300 feet above sea level.

GEOGRAPHIC GENERALITIES

OREGON'S COASTLINE, LAKES AND RIVERS

Coastal Facts
Oregon has approximately 296 miles of coastline.

There are 1853 rocks and islands along the Oregon coast that remain above the water at high tide. Hundreds more surface during low tide.

Depoe Bay is the smallest navigable harbor in the world.

Boiler Bay takes its name from a ship's boiler that can be seen on the beach at low tide. The boiler came from the steam schooner *J. Marhoffer* that exploded and burned nearby in 1910.

The 800-foot-high Cape Perpetua at Yachats is the highest point on Oregon's coast.

River Island
The largest non-delta river island in the world is Oregon's Sauvie Island. Ten miles northwest of Portland, it measures 32.75 square miles, is home to about 1100 people and is the largest island in the Columbia River.

Columbia River

The Columbia is Oregon's largest river. From its headwaters in the Canadian Rockies to the Pacific Ocean, the Columbia travels 1243 miles. The lengths of the other four major rivers are:

Snake	1038 miles
Willamette	309 miles
John Day	281 miles
Klamath	250 miles

Longest River

The two longest rivers contained entirely within the state are the Willamette and the John Day.

Shortest River

The D River connecting Devils Lake with the Pacific Ocean near Lincoln City is the shortest river in Oregon. Depending on the time of day, it's also the shortest river in the world! Although typically listed as being 120 feet long, the D is much longer when the tide is out, which means that the 200-foot Roe River in Montana is sometimes shorter. Since the length of the D River varies so much, the *Guinness Book of World Records* has given the title of shortest river to the Roe.

DID YOU  KNOW?

A nationwide contest was held in 1940 to come up with a new name for Oregon's shortest river. Entries came in from as far away as Australia. Johanna Read of Albany won for suggesting "D River" since all of the river's previous names—Devils Creek, Delake Creek, "the channel to Devils Lake" and the "mouth of Devils Lake"—began with the letter "D."

Scenic River

The John Day River has more miles designated wild and scenic locations by the U.S. Department of Agriculture than any other river in the United States.

OREGON'S AWESOME! Devils Lake, located near Lincoln City, is four-tenths of a mile wide, three miles long and has a maximum depth of only 22 feet. During the winter, it has the greatest diversity of waterfowl anywhere on the Oregon Coast. It is also home to nine species of freshwater fish and the second home of hundreds of fishermen, windsurfers, water skiers and jet skiers. But something else may also live there.

In Chinook Jargon, the place was called *me-sah-chie-chuck*, which means "evil water," and there are many Native American stories about malign spirits and creatures inhabiting the lake's beautiful turquoise waters. For instance, there's one tale of a canoe full of warriors pulled underwater by a huge monster's tentacles. Even today, feasts and sacrifices are held every year on the shores of Devils Lake to placate the beast.

GEOGRAPHIC GENERALITIES

It's Called What?

Stinkingwater Creek, between Drewsey and Malheur Lake, as well as Lake County's Stinkingwater Pass and Nasty Pond, all take their names from the unpleasant aroma of nearby mineral springs.

A Benton County slaughterhouse near Wren used to dump its waste into a neighboring stream. Hence, the name, Greasy Creek.

A creamery in Philomath once dumped its excess buttermilk into what is now called Buttermilk Creek. In the hot weather, an unpleasant odor resulted and the neighbors complained, but the smell only went away when the creamery went out of business.

The Donner und Blitzen River's name has nothing to do with Christmas. In 1864, U.S. Army Captain George Curry and his troops were crossing the river, when they were caught in a raging thunderstorm. *Donner und Blitzen* is German for "thunder and lightning." Locals call the river the Blitzen.

During an 1853 skirmish in the Rogue River Wars, militiaman James Mace lost his pistol in a river along Oregon's southern coast. The river and the nearby town have both been known as Pistol River ever since.

Slab Creek empties into the Pacific Ocean near the town of Neskowin. It takes its name from the slabs of lumber found along the beach after a cargo shipwrecked there in the 1880s. Don't look for it on the map, though! Although local residents still use the original name, it was officially renamed Neskowin Creek in 1925 by the U.S. Bureau of Geographical Names.

A state law was enacted in 1907 that required sheep to be dipped every year in huge vats of chemicals to fight disease. The process required lots of water and, as a result, there are many Dipping Vat Creeks across eastern Oregon.

A hunter in the 1880s looked down into a canyon in Wallowa County and saw a person jumping up and down and hollering like a mad man. Turns out that the guy was just lonely and happy to see another human being! But the stream that flows down that canyon has been known as Crazyman Creek ever since.

Just east of Burns is Poison Creek. It got its name because cattle were poisoned nearby when they ate some wild parsnips.

Another creek in Wallowa County also has a peculiar name. Poker Bill Spring was named in honor of a cowboy, William Tibbetts, who lost everything but a dollar coin in a poker game. While taking a snooze, the dollar fell out of Bill's pocket. But in a stroke of luck, Tibbetts found the money and used it to recover his losses.

OREGON'S AWESOME! There are approximately 1780 natural lakes in Oregon as well as another 4600 ponds, marshes, sloughs and reservoirs. Only a quarter of them have names. Of those that do, 13 are called Lost Lake. There are also 11 Blue Lakes, 10 Clear Lakes and 10 Fish Lakes in the state.

Oregon's Biggest Lake

Upper Klamath Lake covers about 92 square miles, which makes it bigger than the 77-square-mile Malheur Lake. But Malheur Lake, which is actually a giant freshwater marsh, is only eight feet deep, and the land around it is so flat that, if the surface of the lake rises by only a foot—which it often does after a heavy rainfall—its surface area doubles in size!

After heavy rains in 1984, Malheur Lake grew so much that it joined with Harney Lake and Mud Lake to create one giant body of water that covered 280 square miles! As a result, Malheur Lake was bigger than Upper Klamath Lake for most of the 1980s.

Oregon's Great Salt Lakes

The 55-square-mile Lake Abert is the third largest saltwater lake in the United States. Nearby Summer Lake is about 40 square miles. The size of the lakes varies widely in response to rainfall, and in times of drought, both have entirely dried up!

Both lakes were once part of an even larger body of water called Lake Chewaucan, which, 30,000 years ago, covered approximately 460 square miles! From 8000 to 10,000 years ago, its waters started to recede, leaving the two lakes we have today. Fossils of bison, horses, camels and elephants that lived along the ancient shores of Lake Chewaucan can easily be found today.

DID YOU  KNOW?

The 1440-acre Timothy Lake in Clackamas County was once Timothy Meadows. The meadow was purposely flooded in 1956, when the Portland General Electric Company constructed a compacted earth dam along the Clackamas River for hydroelectric power.

Where the Bulls Ran

Portland's vast water reservoir, Bull Run, is named for the wild cattle that escaped from their owners and roamed in the area and not for the Civil War battles.

That's One Big Boo-Boo!

In Lane County, there is a lake that was once accidentally stocked with trout. Hence its name, Boo Boo Lake.

Borax

Just south of Alvord Lake is a small, 10-acre body of water called Borax Lake. It is located near a refining plant where borax was mined and then shipped by mule to Winemucca, Nevada at the beginning of the 20th century.

DID YOU  KNOW?

Borax Lake is the only place in the world where you can find the rare dwarf Borax Lake chub. In fact, it's the only fish in the lake. The lake used to be called Hot Lake because of its warm temperatures. Fed by thermal springs, the average temperature ranges from 61°F to 95°F. Parts of it are as hot as 105°F! As well, the lake naturally contains extremely high levels of arsenic.

Waterfall Wonderland

There are over 700 waterfalls in Oregon. More than 400 of them are in the Oregon Cascades, and 84 are along the 75-mile-long Columbia Gorge between Portland and The Dalles. The highest concentration of waterfalls in the world is found in the 15 miles between Ainsworth State Park and Crown Point State Park. The famous Multnomah Falls is among them.

Multnomah Falls

The Multnomah Falls measures 620 feet from top to bottom, making it the highest waterfall in Oregon and the second highest in the United States. The falls are fed by underground springs on Larch Mountain. A nearby lodge welcomes nearly two million visitors every year, making the site Oregon's second most popular tourist destination. (It was number one until the Spirit Mountain Casino was built in 1998.)

GEOGRAPHIC GENERALITIES

VOLCANOES

America's Volcanic Hotspot

According to the Smithsonian, Oregon has 21 active volcanoes, more than any other state in the continental United States. They include Mount Hood, Mount Bachelor, Mount Jefferson, Mount Mazama or Crater Lake, South Sister or Mount Charity (of the Three Sisters) and Newberry Crater (near Bend). But since Mount McLoughlin has recently given signs that it is alive and well, the number may have to be changed to 22!

The "Most Dangerous" List

In 2006, the U.S. Geological Survey issued a report warning that 18 of America's 169 active volcanoes have a "very high threat" of eruption. That's the USGS's highest danger level. Four of Oregon's volcanoes are on that list: Mount Hood (fourth), South Sister (sixth), Crater Lake (10th) and Newberry Crater (17th).

Danger Within Sight of Portland

Mount Hood has a history of repeated eruptions over long periods of time. The last such series of explosions lasted about 70 years and ended in 1805, just before Lewis and Clark arrived in Oregon. Nothing major has happened since, but there were minor eruptions in 1865 and 1903. And sporadic earthquakes do remind us that the volcano is still alive.

Just How Big a Danger?

Mount Hood is only 46 miles from Portland, but it is unlikely that an eruption would have serious consequences for Oregon's largest city, because the volcano does not have a history of explosive eruptions. Also, most of its past eruptions involved lava flows that traveled only six to eight miles. The bigger danger would be for cities and towns that are downstream from it: past eruptions sent hot gas and avalanches of debris down nearby river basins. The city of Hood River is actually built on the debris pile from an eruption that occurred 50,000 to 100,000 years ago.

OREGON'S AWESOME! There are only two cities in the continental United States that have extinct volcanoes entirely within their city limits, and both of them are in Oregon! One of the volcanoes is Pilot Butte in Bend. Portland has the other three: Mount Tabor, Powell Butte and Rocky Butte. They're all extinct cinder cone volcanoes, which means that the mounds that now exist were built up from the cinders of past eruptions.

DID YOU  KNOW?

Mount Tabor is the only volcano in the world with a basketball court and an outdoor amphitheater. A nearby parking lot needed to be paved, so half the cone was taken away and its cinders were used to make the pavement. Rather than just leave a big, ugly hole, it was decided to make good use of what was left behind.

Crater Lake

Crater Lake sits atop an ancient volcano, now called Mount Mazama. It blew itself up about 6800 years ago in an eruption that was 42 times more powerful than the 1980 eruption of Mount St. Helens. Mazama's magma chamber was emptied during the eruption, and the top of the volcano collapsed, forming a six-mile wide, 3000-feet-deep, bowl-shaped depression known as a caldera. Over the centuries, rain and snow have filled in most of the caldera, forming Crater Lake.

Ash from Mazama's eruption was thrown five to 10 miles into the sky at twice the speed of sound! Today, that ash can be found in eight states and three Canadian provinces. Some 5000 square miles was covered by as much as six inches of the stuff. In the Crater Lake National Park, there are places still covered by 50 feet of ash! Super-heated gas from the explosion traveled 40 miles down the Rogue River Valley and as far north as Diamond Lake.

Before and After

Before the explosion that created Crater Lake, Mount Mazama was approximately 12,000 feet high. That's taller than the highest point in present-day Oregon, Mount Hood, which is only 11,239 feet tall! Today, Mount Scott is the highest remnant of this ancient volcano. Located about two miles from Crater Lake, its peak is only 8929 feet above sea level. Hickman Peak, the highest point on the rim of the lake, measures only 8151 feet. Crater Lake sits 6176 feet above sea level.

Crater Lake is the deepest lake in the United States. It is also the second deepest in the Western Hemisphere and the seventh deepest in the world. Six miles wide, its intense blue color occurs because 100 percent of its water is from rain and snowfall. Because no fish lived in the lake until people brought them there in 1888, there is little sediment, organic material or pollution, and visitors can see an astounding 134 feet into its depths.

War Between the Gods
A local Native American legend about a great battle between two gods developed from the eruption of Mount Mazama. According to the story, Llao of the Below World and Skell of the Above World fought until Llao's home on Mount Mazama was destroyed. Crater Lake, which was supposedly created by the battle, was viewed as a place of danger and supernatural power and was believed to be inhabited by dangerous beings. Shamans prohibited most Native Americans from seeing the lake, and nothing was ever said about it to the fur trappers, miners and settlers who came to southern Oregon in the early 19th century. That's why Crater Lake was not "discovered" until 1853.

A Volcano That Looks Like a Fort?

In the Fort Rock State Park, you'll find an enormous ring of rock resembling a citadel. It is 325 feet high and almost one mile in diameter. It was formed tens of thousands of years ago when magma from a shield volcano erupted into a now-vanished 600-square-mile, 50-foot-deep inland sea. When the magma rose to the surface and met the muddy bottom of the ocean, explosions of hot steam threw the molten material into the air, which then fell back down to form a ring of ash around the vent of the volcano. Eventually, the ring formed an island that stood as tall as a modern skyscraper. There are about 40 other rock rings in Oregon's Great Basin, but unlike Fort Rock, most of them are heavily eroded.

That's One Big Hole!

About eight miles away from Fort Rock is a big, round depression known as Hole in the Ground. It is the collapsed dome of another extinct volcano. Its floor is 150 feet below the surrounding desert; its rim is 5250 feet in circumference and as high as 215 feet above the local terrain. Unlike the small eruptions that created Fort Rock, at least four major explosions created this depression. They sent boulders up to 26 feet in diameter a distance of over two miles!

GEOGRAPHIC GENERALITIES

GLACIERS, MOUNTAINS AND WHATNOT

Glaciers

There are 35 glaciers in Oregon, and all but one are in the Cascades. Seven other glaciers have melted away since their discovery in the 19th and early 20th centuries. The largest surviving glacier is Collier Glacier, located on the west side of North Sister. In 1910, it covered about four-tenths of a square mile in area but has since shrunk to less than half that size.

Guys and Gals

The Three Sisters is not a single mountain but a group of three 10,000-foot volcanic peaks in the Cascade Range. Only a few miles from each another, they were collectively referred to as Clamite by the local Native Americans and have been known as the Three Sisters by settlers as far back as the early 1840s. Individually, the three mountains today have the uninspiring names of North Sister, Middle Sister and South Sister, but during Oregon's pioneer days, they were known, from north to south, as Mount Faith, Mount Hope and Mount Charity.

It was once thought that the Three Sisters were the remains of one massive volcano, but modern volcanologists have determined that the three each have their own history. Recent earthquakes and bulges in the terrain indicate that the volcanic forces beneath South Sister are still active.

Not to be outdone by Faith, Hope and Charity, there is a mountain near Government Camp known as Tom, Dick and Harry. Actually, it's only a ridge above Mirror Lake, but it is the site of one of the most popular hiking trails in the state.

Humbug
Just south of Port Orford is the 1756-foot-high Humbug Mountain. It was originally called Sugar Loaf Mountain, and some explorers in 1851 wanted to climb its south side. They got instructions on how to get there from Captain William Tichenor, an early settler, but still got lost and ended up on the north side instead. The hikers claimed that Tichenor had lied to them and called the mountain Tichenor's Humbug. The name stuck but was eventually reduced to Humbug Mountain. For his part, the captain said that the hikers disregarded his directions.

Three Finger Jack
Straddling the line between Jefferson and Linn counties is a beautiful but dangerous 7841-foot-high peak known as Three Finger Jack. It was originally called Mount Marion, but the name was changed in the early 20th century in honor of a local trapper named Jack who, of course, had only three fingers.

Heaven or Hell?
Not far from Mount Hood is 4556-foot Preachers Peak and its 3900-foot neighbor, Devils Pulpit.

Pancakes
Around 1910, a company of surveyors tried to figure out what to call a 3605-foot-high flat-top mountain in Grant County. Nothing came to mind, so they asked a local teen, John Westfall, for his ideas. Well, John thought the mountain looked like a stack of pancakes, so Johnny Cake Mountain it was.

It's My Fault!
The largest exposed geological fault in the United States lies about 20 miles north of Lakeview. It is a 30-mile-long, 2500-foot-high, near-vertical slope called Abert Rim that divides the plateau above from Lake Abert and a valley below.

Sand Dunes? In the Desert?

Sand dunes in northern Lake County grow as tall as 60 feet! The sand there is a mixture of ash from the volcanic explosion that created Crater Lake and sediment from an ancient lake. Covering 45 square miles, the Christmas Valley Sand Dunes form the largest moving inland sand dune system in the Pacific Northwest.

Haystack? Which Haystack?
Standing a staggering 235 feet, Haystack Rock near Canyon Beach is frequently hailed as the third largest coastal monolith, or sea stack, in the world. But it's not true! It's not even the third largest in Oregon! The sea stack at Nestussa Bay and two of the three sea stacks that make up the Three Arch Rocks off the coast from Tillamook are all bigger than Cannon Beach's Haystack Rock.

Can't Make It to the Coast?
At the Ainsworth State Park along the Columbia Gorge is the 2000-foot-tall St. Peter's Dome. It's a giant monolith made of lava basalt.

Move Over Old Faithful!

Yellowstone is not the only place in the United States with a continuously spouting geyser. Oregon's Old Perpetual near Lakeview shoots a plume of 200°F water over 60 feet into the air every 90 seconds.

Oregon is also home to Crump Geyser. Located near Adel, it was, for a short time, the largest continually erupting geyser in the United States. The geyser was created accidentally in 1959 when the Magma Power Company drilled a 1680-foot well. Two days later, the geyser spontaneously erupted, sending boiling water 200 feet into the air. This continued, nonstop, for about six months before it naturally became a geyser that spouted at regular intervals. In the early 1960s, someone threw several large boulders into the geyser's casing, and the water now erupts only 58 feet once every two minutes or so.

Scientific research has determined that the local area is part of an extensive underground hot spring system, and the federal government has identified it as a "top pick" for potential geothermal power development. Indeed, Nevada Geothermal Power, Inc., has recently acquired leases on the 6500 acres surrounding the geyser in order to conduct exploration and development.

Please Marry Me

Proposal Rock at the mouth of the Neskowin Creek is one of the Oregon coast's most beautiful sites. It got its name from Mrs. Henry Page, an early local settler, who christened it after her daughter, Della, accepted a proposal of marriage there from Charlie Gage.

Go Into the Ground to Get Ice for Ice Cream

Open cracks or fissures on the earth's surface frequently occur whenever there's an earthquake or volcanic activity. Most quickly disappear when they are filled in with rock or lava. But eight miles north of the town of Christmas Valley is a two-mile-long fissure called Crack in the Ground. It ranges from 10 to 15 feet wide and 10 to 70 feet deep and has remained open for 1000 years! People have been exploring the caves inside the crack for years. In fact, locals use the ice found inside the caves year-round to make their ice cream!

Drink the Family?

Drinkwater Pass, east of Drewsey, was named after a local family and not after any water found nearby.

A Place of Ill Repute

Near Frenchglen, one mile east of Fish Lake, is Whorehouse Meadows. Back in the Old West, entrepreneurs of the oldest profession set up canvas tents and catered to the needs of the local cattlemen and sheepherders. The U.S. Bureau of Land Management thought a less bawdy name was warranted and tried to change it in the 1960s to Naughty Girl Meadows, but the public and the Oregon Geographic Names Board strongly objected, so the original moniker was reinstated in 1981.

Propeller Meadows

In 1945, a B-24 on a training flight crashed into a peak of the Pueblo Mountains near Denio just north of the Oregon-Nevada border. All 11 on board died. Exactly what happened remains a mystery. The weather was clear, there was no distress call and witnesses say that the plane's engines sounded just fine as it flew overhead. And, yet, the bomber hit a rocky outcrop at full speed. Most of the wreckage was buried at the site, but some, including the propellers, remain scattered over the area as a memorial to the airmen who were killed. The site is known as Propeller Meadows.

ENVIRONMENT

FOREST LANDS

Oregon has 32 million acres of forested land, which means that 51.3 percent of the state is covered by trees! That's one-tenth of all the forested land in the country! No wonder Oregon is America's leading provider of lumber.

According to the Oregon Department of Forestry, here are the types of trees you'll find in the state's forests:

Type of tree	Area covered in acres
Ponderosa pine	7,040,042
Douglas fir	6,985,074
Douglas fir/mixed conifer	3,680,067
Northeast mixed	3,094,618
True fir/mountain hemlock	1,976,328
Regenerating forest	1,844,912
Western mixed	1,679,341
Lodgepole pine/Jeffery pine/subalpine fir	1,024,951
Spruce/hemlock	402,651
Deciduous	270,144

Valley of the Giants

No, it's not some remake of the 1960s science-fiction TV show! It's the name of a 51-acre forest preserve near Falls City established by the U.S. Bureau of Land Management to protect a stand of 400- to 450-year-old giant Douglas fir and hemlock trees. Some of them are 200 feet tall and are over 20 feet in diameter. It's one of the last old-growth tree stands left in Oregon.

More Giants

According to the National Register of Big Trees, Oregon boasts 38 giants that are either the tallest tree of their kind in the United States or sport the widest diameter. Here are a few examples:

- A Rocky Mountain Douglas fir in Deschutes National Forest measures 26 feet 4 inches in circumference and 139 feet tall.

- A tanoak measuring 22 feet 11 inches in circumference and a towering 144 feet in height is located near Ophir.

- A Port Orford cedar measuring 219 feet high and 37 feet 7 inches in circumference is located in the Siskiyou National Forest.

- A Sitka spruce measuring 56 feet 1 inch in circumference and 206 feet tall is located at Klootchy Creek Park in Clatsop County.

A Tiny Giant

Finally, at only 22 feet tall, a silver buffaloberry shrub found in Malheur County may not seem that impressive, but the shrubs normally grow no higher than 14 feet, making it a real giant!

The Klootchy Creek Giant

Oregon's most famous Sitka spruce is called the Klootchy Creek Giant. The 206-foot tree has lived for 500 to 750 years but, unfortunately, its days are numbered. It is rotten inside, and a December storm in 2006 tore away a part of its trunk where an old lightening scar used to be. Arborists say that will live another 10 years at most.

DID YOU KNOW?

The Klootchy Creek Giant contains enough wood to build 42 small, three-bedroom houses.

ENVIRONMENT

How Do You Lose A Forest?

In the eastern part of the desert in Christmas Valley are 9000 acres of ponderosa pine and juniper trees known as the Lost Forest. Thirty-five miles from any other forest, it has survived despite conditions dry enough to kill the trees because it sits on top of a unique mixture of sand, minerals and volcanic pumice that acts like a giant sponge. Even so, scientists say the trees are starting to die from lack of water.

DID YOU  KNOW?

The largest juniper tree in Oregon (78 feet tall and 6.2 feet in diameter) is in the Lost Forest.

Two Ghost Forests

At low tide, not far from Neskowin, submerged tree stumps appear when the sand has been washed away. The stumps were seen for the first time in 1997 and were, for a short while, a bit of a mystery. Radiocarbon dating indicates they're between 1700 and 2000 years old. It's believed that a massive earthquake dropped an ancient forest into the ocean. When a tsunami caused by the quake hit the shore, the tops of the trees were lopped off, leaving the stumps to be buried and preserved in the mud and sand.

Another ghost forest was discovered on a seaside cliff between Yachats and Cape Perpetua in 2005 and presents a bigger mystery: radiocarbon dating indicates that the trees died at least 55,000 years ago, but that is as far back as that dating technique can go with any degree of accuracy. So, one expert suggests that the trees may actually be 80,000 or 100,000 years old! The trees were flattened in a massive landslide and then buried in sediment that protected them from decay.

ENVIRONMENT

Largest Cypress in the World?
The largest Monterey cypress tree in Oregon is on the grounds of the Chetco Valley Museum in Harbor. Some say that it's the largest in the world. The tree is 99 feet high and 27 feet in diameter.

DID YOU KNOW?

The largest forest of ponderosa pine in the United States is located in Oregon's Grant and Harney counties.

The Birth of Oregon's Orchards
Henderson Leuelling carried apple, cherry, pear, plum and black walnut trees with him on his first journey west in 1846. He also brought along some currant, gooseberry, grape, quince and hickory plants. They all took to Oregon's soil and climate, making Luelling—and generations of farmers—very prosperous indeed!

Heritage Trees

Ever since 1995, the Travel Information Council has identified and designated 32 Oregon Heritage Trees across the state in the hope of increasing the public's awareness of the important role that trees have played in the state's history and in maintaining our quality of life.

DID YOU KNOW?

Oregon's first Heritage Tree was the Ewing Young Oak in Newberg. Designated a Heritage Tree in 1995, the acorn from which it grew was planted over Young's grave in 1846. Young was a wealthy early settler who died 1841 without a wife or children. Without a legally organized government in Oregon, his neighbors weren't sure what to do with his property. Their dilemma led directly to the establishment of Oregon's provisional government in 1843.

ENVIRONMENT

CONSERVATION AND PARKLANDS

King of Conservation
Samuel H. Boardman became Oregon's first state parks superintendent in 1929 and filled the post for 21 years. With an eye for conservation and a desire to maintain Oregon's natural beauty, Boardman's efforts at acquiring land resulted in a state park system that grew from an initial 4000 acres to more than 60,000 acres by the time he retired.

There are more than 174 parks, viewpoints, recreational sites and trails in Oregon. These include 14 national forests, three national monuments, three national parks, two national recreation areas, one national scenic area, three national trails and 21 national wildlife refuges

Like to Hike?
The Oregon Trail Advisory Council maintains 16 historic trails recognized for their historic value. The Lewis and Clark, the Oregon, the Applegate and the Nez Perce National Historic Trails are the most famous.

Three Arch Rocks
One of the best-known landmarks on the Oregon Coast, the Three Arch Rocks National Wildlife Refuge is half a mile offshore from Oceanside. It consists of three large and six smaller rocks that stick straight out of the ocean. Established in 1907, the refuge is the oldest National Wildlife Refuge west of the Mississippi River and, with over 250,000 birds, is home to the largest nesting bird colony in the state. It is also the only pupping site on the northern Oregon Coast for the endangered Steller sea lion.

Eagle Cap

The largest federal wilderness area in Oregon is the Eagle Cap Wilderness Area 30 miles east of La Grande. Its 350,000 acres contain 53 alpine lakes and 534 miles of trails, some of which are up to 43 miles long! Eagle Cap has an elevation of 9595 feet.

Blind Park

The 23-acre Oral Hull Park near Sandy is designed as a park for the blind. Signs are in braille, and the hiking trails and walking paths are lined with waist-high railings and guide wires. There is also a swimming pool, hot tub, a pond stocked with trout and a lodge.

Flush Toilets!

Built in 1915, the Eagle Creek Campground between Bonneville Dam and Cascade Locks was the first U.S. Forest Service campground in the country. When it was renovated in the 1930s, the first flush toilet at a forest service facility was installed. And the toilet is still being used!

ENVIRONMENT

OUR FLYING FRIENDS

Bald Eagle Country

The Klamath Basin in south-central Oregon and northern California has the largest concentration of wintering bald eagles in the continental United States: in winter there are between 600 and 1000! Over 200 nesting pairs have been documented. Eagles are frequently seen on the Oregon coast and on the western side of the Cascade Mountains.

DID YOU  KNOW?

Over one million seabirds, including auklets, cormorants, guillemots, murres, pelicans, petrels and puffins nest every year along Oregon's coast. That's more than all the birds that nest off the California and Washington coasts combined!

That's Some Bird

Fifty thousand storm petrels nest in burrows on Saddle Rock Island off Crook Point. These tiny birds only go out at night and fly as far as 200 miles out to sea to catch food for their young.

DID YOU  KNOW?

Malheur Lake is the site of the largest concentration of nesting inland water birds in the state. Over one million bitterns, cranes, egrets, grebes and other birds call Malheur Lake and nearby Harney Lake home during their nesting season.

Environmental Protection

Oregon has long been a pioneer in the environmental movement. For example:

- In 1971, Oregon was the first state to adopt a law that gave refunds for returned glass and aluminum bottles and cans.

- In 1979, Oregon became the first state to require timber companies to replant logged-out forests with new trees.

Tougher Than Kyoto

In 1993, Portland's city council became the first local government in the United States to adopt a plan to address global warming. Its strategy contains more than 100 steps designed to reduce overall greenhouse gas emissions in the Rose City to 10 percent below its 1990 levels by 2010. (The Kyoto Protocol calls for only a seven percent reduction.) And guess what? It's working! Portland reached its 1990 emission levels in 2004, and they're still dropping. It is also estimated that, thanks to the plan (which Multnomah County signed onto in 2001), emissions are down 17 percent from what they would have been if nothing had been done at all. Since 1993, 131 other cities have adopted plans to meet the goals of the Kyoto Protocol, including Corvallis and Eugene.

POPULATION

BY THE NUMBERS

Head Count

According to the U.S. Census, 3.5 million people lived in Oregon in 2000. By 2006, that number increased to 3.7 million. Oregon ranks 28th among the states by population.

How Old are Oregon's Residents?

- 6.3 percent are under five years of age
- 23.7 percent are under 18 years of age
- 63.5 percent are between 18 and 65
- 12.8 percent are 65 years and older
- The median age is 36.3 years

Who are They?

- 49.7 percent are male
- 50.3 percent are female
- 82 percent are white, non-Hispanic
- 9.5 percent are Hispanic or Latino
- 1.8 percent are African American
- 1.4 percent are Native American or Alaska Native
- 3.4 percent are of Asian descent
- 0.3 percent are Native Hawaiian or other Pacific Islander
- 2.3 percent are of two or more races

Connected?

Seventy-seven percent of all of Oregon's households have personal computers, and 67 percent have high-speed Internet access.

Sensational Census

Oregon first participated in the federal census in 1850 when it was still a territory. At that time, 13,294 people lived in Oregon, but it then included Washington, Idaho and parts of Montana and Wyoming. Only 12,093 were living within Oregon's current borders. Native Americans were not counted since they were not yet American citizens. Oregon's first federal census as a state was taken in 1860. The population that year was 52,465.

Between 1860 and 2000, Oregon's population has tended to double every 28.8 years. During the same period, the number of people who call Oregon home has increased 6421 percent!

Oregon's estimated population in July 2006 was 3,700,758. That's an 8.62 percent increase in only six years!

POPULATION

National Population Ranking

State	Population ranking	Population numbers
California	1st	33,871,648
Washington	15th	5,894,121
Oregon	28th	3,421,399
Nevada	35th	1,998,257
Idaho	39th	1,293,953

What Does the Future Hold?
While it is impossible to accurately predict population growth, the U.S. Census Bureau says that, by 2015, Oregon's population will be about 4 million and, by 2025, 4.35 million. That's the 12th fastest projected rate of growth in the country!

DID YOU KNOW?

The Willamette Valley is 120 miles long, 20 to 40 miles wide and stretches from Cottage Grove to the junction of the Willamette and Columbia Rivers. It is home to 2.3 million Oregonians, which is approximately two-thirds of Oregon's residents. It's the fastest growing region in the state, and eight of Oregon's 10 largest cities are located there: only Bend and Medford are found elsewhere. It is anticipated that another 1.7 million people (for a total of four million) will be living in the valley by 2050. That's the equivalent of adding three cities the size of present-day Portland!

POPULATION

The Aging of Oregon
In 2000, approximately 13 percent of Oregonians were 65 years of age or older. But according to the experts, that number will be more than 25 percent by 2050.

Quick Health Facts

☛ On average, Oregonians live 78 years.

☛ 15.6 percent of Oregonians have no health insurance.

☛ 11.2 percent of Oregonians are enrolled in the Oregon Health Plan.

- 18 percent of Oregonians suffer from a long-lasting disability.
- 21 percent of Oregonians were considered obese in 2005, nearly double the 1990 rate. That's lower than the national rate of 24.5 percent, but higher than nearby Montana's 19.1 percent.
- The obesity rate in Oregon did not increase in 2004–05, making it the only state in the country where the rate did not go up.
- It is estimated that, in 2003, $781 million was spent on treating problems caused by obesity.
- The oldest hospital in Oregon is Portland's Providence St. Vincent Medical Center. It opened as the St. Vincent Hospital in 1875. There are now 91 hospitals in the state.

What State Are You From?

Of the 1,556,490 Oregon residents (2000 census) who were born elsewhere in the United States, 443,276 were born in California and 190,295 in Washington.

Other Top States of Origin

Idaho	57,069
Illinois	51,016
Texas	48,934
New York	44,453
Minnesota	41,868
Colorado	35,649
Montana	33,729
Oklahoma	32,996

POPULATION

And the Top 10 Are!

What about foreign-born Oregonians? The top 10 countries listed as their places of birth and the number of residents who were born there are:

Mexico	113,083
Canada	17,137
Vietnam	16,523
Russia / Soviet Union	14,032
China (including Hong Kong and Taiwan)	11,641
Korea	10,488
Germany	8568
Philippines	7474
India	6866
Japan	6351

Please Visit, But Don't Stay!

"Come visit us again and again. This is a state of excitement. But for heaven's sake, don't move here to live." (Governor Tom McCall, 1971) Ironically, McCall was born in Massachusetts.

Please Don't Go!!!

As of 2000, 796,977 people born in Oregon now live elsewhere in the United States, but most of them haven't moved far away. Fifty-nine percent—473,479—now reside in California, Idaho, or Washington.

POPULATION

Leaving Home
The top 10 destinations for Oregonians who move out of state are:

Washington	249,494
California	176,433
Idaho	47,522
Arizona	33,311
Texas	26,547
Nevada	21,112
Colorado	20,262
Alaska	19,235
Utah	15,858
Florida	13,812

Citizens of Atlantis?
According to the 2000 census, there are presently three Oregonians who were born at sea to non-American parents!

Where Were Your Ancestors From?

According to the 2000 census, 20.9 percent of Oregonians brag of ancestors from Germany, making German the largest ancestry group in the state. The four other large ancestry groups are:

English	13.2 percent
Irish	11.9 percent
American	6.2 percent
Mexican	5.5 percent

Melting Pot

People of German ancestry make up the largest part of the population in 29 of Oregon's 36 counties. However, in Baker County, the plurality claim English descent. Native Americans are among the largest groups in Jefferson county. In Hood River, Malheur and Morrow counties, more residents are of Mexican background than of any other. And, in Crook County, the plurality identify themselves as being of "American" descent.

Little Ireland

So many people from the Emerald Isle immigrated to Lake County during its early years that many today call it "Little Ireland." The county seat, Lakeview, once had a newspaper called *The Irish News* that catered to the "Irish Citizens of Lake County" and was home to the only all-Irish civic organization in Oregon. The Irish Room at the Lake County Museum is the only permanent Irish museum in the state.

What Language Do You Speak?

According to the 2000 census, 12.1 percent of Oregonians who are age five or older speak a language other than English at home, less than the national average of 17.9 percent.

Most of them speak Spanish, but German, Vietnamese, Russian and Chinese are also common.

No Particular Church

Compared to the rest of the country, Oregon has the highest number of folks who identify themselves as non-religious or who claim a personal faith without subscribing to a particular church or religious group—17 percent of the population.

POPULATION

Faith

Only 12 percent of Oregonians identify themselves as active members of a church. That's the lowest rate of church membership in the United States. Christianity is Oregon's largest religion. The most popular denominations are the Roman Catholic Church, the Church of Jesus Christ of Latter-day Saints and the Evangelical Lutheran Church in America.

DID YOU  KNOW?

Judaism is the most popular non-Christian faith in America. But not in Oregon! Here, 0.5 percent of the population are Buddhist; only 0.38 percent are Jewish.

Thinking Outside the Box

Oregon's reputation for religious tolerance has meant groups such as the Neo-Pagan and Wiccan communities have small but established groups in the state. The Wiccan faith is the fastest growing faith in the United States. Some interesting tidbits about some of Oregon's other faiths:

- Members of the Breitenbush Community, established in Detroit, Oregon, in 1991, live and work in an "eco-village" that offers visitors everything from yoga to a traditional sweat lodge.

- The Old Believers are a branch of the Russian Orthodox faith and adhere to early church teachings, speak Russian between themselves and dress according to 17th century styles.

- The first American members of Sun Myung Moon's Unification Church organized themselves in Eugene back in 1959.

- The Fellowship of Urantia Book Readers was founded in 1955 to study the Urantia Book. The book was first published in English in 1955 in Eugene, and its more than 2000 pages are said to record the subconscious knowledge of a psychiatric patient cared for by Dr. William S. Sadler in Chicago from 1934 to 1935.

Contentious Community

One of Oregon's religious communities left a black mark on the state's history. In 1981, East Indian guru Bhagwan Shree Rajneesh left India and established a 64,000-acre commune 10 miles from Antelope that included everything from a 4500-foot-long paved airstrip to an 88,000-square-foot meeting hall. Eventually, 7000 followers lived there. Tensions with the locals were high. Not only did the Bhagwan fail to apply for building permits, he attempted to bring the world's homeless to his ranch and pushed the county government to provide them with the right to vote.

Then in 1985, Rajneesh's secretary was charged with theft and attempted murder after spreading salmonella bacteria over a restaurant salad bar. More than 750 people in The Dalles were infected. The Bhagwan was eventually indicted on federal immigration charges and deported to India. His ranch was sold and today is used as a Christian youth camp.

POPULATION
NATIVE AMERICANS

Tribes Old and New
Beginning in 1776, the United States maintained a special relationship with the Native American tribes through statutes, agreements and treaties. But in the 1950s, Congress passed laws that terminated the special status of 109 tribes and bands across the United States. Sixty-two of them were in Oregon.

Since the 1970s, many Native Americans have succeeded in restoring their tribal governments. The first in Oregon to successfully achieve federal restoration were the Siletz in 1977, and others have followed. However, these newly recognized tribes and their reservations often combine the descendants of separate tribes.

The Native Population
According to the 2000 census, the total population of Native Americans in Oregon is 48,341. And although they are only 1.14 percent of Oregon's residents, the state ranks 11th among those with the highest proportion of Native Americans in its population. There are currently 10 federally recognized tribes in Oregon.

Reservation Lands
There are five Native American reservations in Oregon:

Reservation	Size (Acres)	First Established
Siletz	3200	1855
Grand Ronde	33,148	1855
Umatilla	79,820	1855
Warm Springs	322,108	1855
Klamath	872,186	1864

 The 61-acre Indian Mary Park is described as the "crown jewel" of Josephine County's park system, and was once the smallest reservation in the United States!

In 1855, a Native American, Umpqua Jack, warned miners and settlers along the Rogue River of an impending attack. In gratitude for what he had done, Umpqua Jack and his wife and family were allowed to live on the site of the present-day park. In 1894, his daughter obtained a 25-year deed to the land, making it the smallest reservation in the country.

Native American Place Names

Ten Oregon counties, a large number of cities and towns, and hundreds of rivers, lakes, mountains and other places of interest are named after famous Native Americans or their tribes. Many others use local Native American words for their names.

Examples include:

Clackamas	Umatilla
Clatsop	Wallowa
Coos	Wasco
Klamath	Yamhill
Multnomah	Umpqua
Tillamook	Yachtas

POPULATION

FRENCH CANADIANS

Oregon's *Coureurs de Bois*

In the early 19th century, the Hudson's Bay Company and its competitor, the North West Company, employed many French-Canadian trappers—the *coureurs de bois*—who traveled all across Oregon in search of beaver pelts. In fact, there were so many of them that the main language used at the Bay Company's Fort Vancouver in present-day Vancouver, Washington, was French.

DID YOU  KNOW?

The first permanent settlers in the Willamette Valley were French-Canadians who decided to stay and establish farms in Oregon after they retired from the fur trade. Most settled at French Prairie in northern Marion County.

The French-Canadian Heritage

Almost 31,000 Oregonians claim French Canadian ancestry. The importance of Oregon's French-Canadian heritage is reflected in the names of Deschutes and Malheur counties as well as in the names of cities such as Gervais, Grand Ronde, La Grande and The Dalles.

Don't Make Assumptions!

Frenchglen's name has nothing to do with the French Canadians who roamed Oregon's wilderness looking for beaver. It's named after two early settlers—Peter French and Hugh Glenn.

TOURISM AND TRIVIA

ROADSIDE ATTRACTIONS

Shoe Tree?

The Juntura Shoe Tree began with a single dreamer tossing a pair of sneakers, tied together by their shoelaces, onto a branch. Over time, travelers and locals added their own, until today there are so many shoes on the tree that the branches are starting to sway under the weight. There are other shoe trees in Idaho, Indiana, Maine, Atlanta, Michigan, New York, California and Nevada.

A 17-foot fiberglass caveman in Grants Pass, complete with club and loincloth was erected in 1971 to commemorate a local tradition dating back to 1922: shopkeepers march down Main Street wearing animal skins and dragging ceremonial clubs to boost business. The tradition continues today!

A 29-foot black bird with an oversized beak and foreboding claws overlooks the parking lot of the Black Bird Auto and Hardware Store in Medford.

A 21-foot-tall, 35-foot-wide concrete candle stands in front of the Damascus firehall. It's a replica of the Oregon Centennial Candle, made in 1959, which was supposed to burn for eternity. However, it had to be put out after only 100 days when its sponsor ran out of money.

Twenty-three life-sized dinosaur replicas grace a walking trail that winds its way through the Oregon rain forest at Port Orford's Prehistoric Gardens.

A 31-foot-tall replica of the Statue of Liberty sits on top of a brick pedestal at the DP Auto Service in Milwaukie. There was a little problem during the statute's installation in 2006—the head caught on fire—but everything is okay now.

Look Up—Way Up
On the Tualatin Valley Highway near Aloha, a 15-foot-tall half human-half bunny named Harvey the Giant Rabbit stands just outside Harvey Marine, a marine supply store. He's made from an abandoned fiberglass service station mascot and a bunny head. Passersby honk their horns when they see him, and when locals heard that one of Harvey's ears had been stolen by vandals, the shop was inundated with get-well wishes!

Bomber Gas

An 18-ton, 75-foot-long B-17G "Flying Fortress" with a nearly 104-foot wingspan sits at a former gas station in Milwaukie, Oregon. The bomber was built in 1944 for $350,000, but was surplussed after World War II. Milwaukie pilot and entrepreneur Art Lacey bought it for only $13,750 in 1947 and flew it from Oklahoma to Oregon to place it over his gas station.

A huge success, the Bomber Gas Station eventually had 40 gas pumps and was one of the largest stations in the United States. The Bomber Drive-In restaurant opened next door in 1948. The gas station closed in 1991, but the restaurant continues to serve Bomber Burgers.

OREGON'S AWESOME! At Deschutes Junction near Bend is the Funny Farm. Part antique store, part animal shelter and part park and playground, its unusual displays include the Yellow Brick Road of *Wizard of Oz* fame, the Agitator Wall created from washing-machine parts, a pink flamingo nesting area and a totem pole made of tires. Its most recent addition is a one-ton bowling ball tree. There's the heart-shaped Love Pond where, on the last Saturday of every year, couples can be married for free. (The site is also available for weddings the rest of the year for a small fee.) And where else can you buy high-quality hybrid bowling ball seeds or a book entitled *How to Cook Bowling Balls*?

Norman? Are You Here?

There's a Bates Motel in Vale. It doesn't look a thing like the one in the movie *Psycho*, but that doesn't keep tourists from stopping and making it one of the most photographed motels in the world.

Wonderland

The Enchanted Forest south of Salem started out as a storybook fantasyland for founder Roger Tofte's own children. It grew into a full-scale theme park with everything from a western town and traditional English village to a haunted house and outdoor theater. The park is open most days from mid-March to the end of September.

LIGHTHOUSES

Leave the Lights On
Oregon's coastline is awash in natural beauty, but sailors spend their time searching out the human-made beauty of the nine lighthouses that dot the landscape. Four have been decommissioned and designated historic monuments, but the others remain in operation.

Rest in Peace
The Tillamook Rock Lighthouse was built on a rock about a mile and a half out to sea off Cannon Beach, so you can't visit it. But you can lay your loved one's ashes to rest there. "Terrible Tilly" was privately purchased in 1980, stripped, sealed shut and converted into the Eternity at Sea Columbarium, a cemetery at sea of sorts, equipped to hold more than 500,000 urns!

Useless (If You're Coming From the North)
The Yaquina Bay Lighthouse, constructed in 1871, is the only surviving wooden lighthouse in Oregon. It's also the only one with the lighthouse keeper's residence attached to the building. In fact, the lantern room containing the light sits right on top of the house! And it's also the oldest building in Newport. Unfortunately, the lighthouse was built on a bluff at the mouth of the Yaquina River and, because of the headlands, its light can't be seen from the north. So it was closed after only three years of operation. The lighthouse was restored to operation in 1996.

The Tallest
The Yaquina Head Lighthouse near Newport is Oregon's tallest lighthouse. Built in 1873, the lighthouse itself is 93 feet tall. Its lantern room is 162 feet above sea level. It took over a year and 370,000 bricks to build. There are 114 steps up the stairway to the top, and you're welcome to give them a try either by yourself or with a tour guide.

TOURISM AND TRIVIA

The Shortest

The shortest lighthouse in Oregon is the Cape Meares Lighthouse near Tillamook. It's only 38 feet high. Fortunately, it sits on top of a 217-foot cliff!

Every lighthouse has a unique flashing pattern. The light warns passing ships of danger, while the pattern indicates the light's location along the coast. For example, the beacon's pattern at the Yaquina Head Lighthouse is two seconds on, two seconds off, two seconds on and then 14 seconds off.

It Played a Role in the Equal Rights Movement

The Cape Blanco Lighthouse near Port Orford was built in 1870 and is Oregon's oldest continuously operating lighthouse. Sitting on land that is 197 feet above sea level, its lantern room is 256 feet in the air, which makes Cape Blanco the highest lighthouse in the state. From that height, its signal can be seen from 22⅔ nautical miles out at sea. It also sits on the most westerly point in the state. But most interestingly, Cape Blanco was where Mabel Bretherton became Oregon's first woman lighthouse keeper in 1903.

At $600 a year, being a lighthouse keeper was one of the best paying jobs in the United States in the 1870s. But look at the job description: a lonely existence on a small island or a ledge of rocks with sea and storm constantly battering at your door and supplies and mail arriving only a few times a year. They earned their money!

Get Married…At a Lighthouse!

Built in 1894, the Heceta Head Lighthouse is said to be the most photographed lighthouse in the country. It's easy to see why once you glimpse its stunning views. In addition, the lighthouse keeper's house is now a bed and breakfast where the cook serves seven-course gourmet breakfasts and four-course dinners. The lighthouse is also a romantic spot where many couples exchange their wedding vows.

TOURISM AND TRIVIA

NATURAL ATTRACTIONS

Mysterious Site
Gold Hill is home to the Oregon Vortex, a place where balls roll uphill and people seem to be standing sideways! How can that be? One theory is that the landscape confuses our eyes and inner ears so that what looks like an incline is actually a decline. Whatever the reason, folks flock to the site to see what all the fuss is about. There are about 15 such sites in North America.

The Sea Lion Caves near Florence are actually one large cavern. At 25 million years old, 310 feet long, 164 feet wide and 12 stories tall, it is the largest sea cave in the world. It is also the only year-round home for wild sea lions on the North American mainland. Two hundred or so Steller sea lions also live there, and California sea lions can be seen from late fall to early spring. Sometimes even a gray whale or two pass by!

Amazing Caves
Although difficult to find, the Arnold Ice Caves, located in the Deschutes National Forest near Bend, are as mysterious as they are wonderful. This eight-mile "ice cave" is actually a lava tube where seasonal ice was once harvested in the early 19th century. It's big enough that horses are allowed inside.

Amazon in Oregon
Cape Perpetua, near Yachats, is a little like the Amazon minus the poisonous plants and snakes. The rain forest there encompasses about 2700 acres of ancient trees, plant life and assorted wildlife.

Celebrated Naturalist

The William L. Finley National Wildlife Refuge in Benton County was established in 1964 as a 5666-acre winter refuge dusky Canada geese, but peregrine falcons and bald eagles have also found the area a safe haven.

A Fossil, Anyone?
The city of Fossil has been known for its fossils ever since its founder, Thomas Hoover, discovered them on his ranch in the early 1890s. When the city of Fossil dug up a hillside to build a football field for the local high school, they discovered an ancient lakebed full of fossilized plants from the Oligocene Period. Their quality is exceptional thanks to the fine volcanic ash that buried the plants millions of years ago. For a $3 fee, you're allowed to take home up to three specimens.

Marble Halls of Oregon
The Oregon Caves east of Cave Junction contain countless stalactites, stalagmites and calcite formations. Tours take guests underground through several caverns and tunnels, including the giant Ghost Room that is 250 feet long, 50 feet wide and 40 feet high. The caves remain a constant 43 degrees all year round. The most complete fossil of a jaguar ever found in the United States was recently found in the caves.

Meteorite Replicas

Stop by the Museum of Natural and Cultural History at the University of Oregon or at the Willamette Methodist Church in West Linn to see their replicas of the Willamette meteorite. The original was discovered near West Linn in 1902. Weighing in at about 32,000 pounds, it is 10 feet tall, 6 feet 6 inches wide and 4 feet 3 inches deep. It's the largest meteorite ever found in the United States and the sixth largest in the world. The original is now at the American Museum of Natural History in New York.

Agates

All sort of things wash up on the beach north of Newport—trash from ships, packing crates, floats, driftwood, shells and fossils. But the most beautiful are the thousands of small translucent stones. These agates are red, blue and amber and come from nearby gravel beds, creeks and cliffs, not the oceans. There are 20 varieties of the stone, and they are found from Florence to Otis. One of the highest concentrations is at Agate Beach.

Blue Cheese, Hot Dogs and Lonely Beaches

Langlois used to be famous for its high-quality blue cheese. A local company made a sweet and creamy cheese from goat's milk, and it was even served at the Waldorf Astoria in New York City. The factory is now gone, but Langlois Market is gaining fame for hot dogs that are topped with a mustard made from a secret recipe. And because tourists have not yet discovered the sand dune that separates Langlois from the ocean, *Sunset Magazine* called it "Oregon's Loneliest Beach."

DID YOU KNOW?

Oregon has two nude beaches that have been officially designated as "clothing-optional." One is Collins Beach on Sauvie Island, and the other is Rooster Rock State Park near Troutdale.

TOURISM AND TRIVIA

ARCHITECTURAL ATTRACTIONS

The Covered Bridge State

There were once about 450 covered bridges in the state! In fact, some say there were as many as 600! All but 51 are now gone, but that's still more than anywhere else west of the Mississippi. There's even a Covered Bridge Society whose members are dedicated to saving the structures that are left.

In Stayton every September, there is a two-day Oregon Covered Bridge Festival, where visitors tour six local bridges and learn about their history. The festival is the only one of its kind in the western United States.

O Pioneers!
The Vista House at Crown Point State Park is a 55-foot-high, octagonal, sandstone-faced structure that resembles a giant thimble! It was built between 1916 and 1918 as a monument to Oregon's pioneers and was intended to promote the use of the Historic Columbia River Highway. Sitting atop a dramatic rock point called "Thor's Crown" some 733 feet above the Columbia River, its design was inspired by the 1896 painting *Valhalla* by Max Bruckner.

Originally budgeted at $17,000, it cost almost $100,000 because Alaskan marble was used in the floors and stairway. When money ran out, the interior of the building's dome was painted to look like marble and copper. Critics have referred to it as "the $100,000 outhouse."

The Watchman

The *Golden Pioneer* stands on top of the Oregon State Capitol. He's 22 feet tall, made of solid bronze and covered in 23K gold leaf. He has been watching over Salem residents since 1938 and was sculpted by Ulric H. Ellerhusen.

Want to Go Skiing?

The Timberline Lodge on Mount Hood is the only ski resort in North America that is open all year-round. Built entirely by hand from massive timbers and native stone, it took 15 months in extreme weather conditions before construction was completed. Four stories high and encompassing 12,350 square feet, the first floor is often covered with snow, and people have been known to ski down the building itself. Dedicated by President Franklin Roosevelt in 1937, Timberline was declared a National Historic Landmark in 1978.

MUSEUMS

Museum Mecca

There are over 200 museums in Oregon and more than 2.5 million guests visit them every year! Most are nonprofit organizations and, on average, 75 percent of their funding comes from admission fees, donations, contributions and other private sources. Some of the more offbeat include:

- ☛ The International Museum of Carousel Art in Hood River started out in the mid-1970s with Carol Perron's desire for one—and only one—carousel horse for her home. Today the museum has more than 110 carved carousel animals, which makes it the largest collection of antique carousel art in the world!

- ☛ The Evergreen Aviation Museum in McMinnville displays the *Spruce Goose*, a huge plane referred to as a "flying boat" that was created and built by Howard Hughes during World War II. There is also an assortment of props from Martin Scorcese's film, *The Aviator*.

- ☛ Portland's Vacuum Museum has 300 vacuums from the wood-made contraptions of the 1800s to the stylish cleaners of the 1960s. Bet you didn't know the first vacuum cleaner was a "sweeping machine" patented in 1869! There's also a Busy Bee that required two people to operate it (one pumped while the other vacuumed) and a Duntley Pneumatic whose suction seal was so strong that salesmen could attach the vacuum to the ceiling and use it to do chin-ups.

- ☛ Portland's Velveteria displays over 200 velvet paintings. There are clowns, children, animals, Liberace, Mexican bandits, South Pacific Islands, nudes, paintings that glow in black light and some that are just weird.

MUSEUMS AND FESTIVALS

- Portland's Hat Museum is the only one of its kind in the United States. The museum's 600 Stetsons, deerstalkers, nurses' caps, souvenir hats, designer hats and more are divided into four collections for the viewer to enjoy. There's even a Thanksgiving hat that sings! You'll also find John Steinbeck's doorstop, a red British telephone booth and a couch made from a Cadillac in the museum.

- Want to see the world's largest hairball? A kidney-shaped, two-pound hairball is on display at one of the two museums at the Mount Angel Abbey and Seminary in St. Benedict. It's seven inches long, three inches wide and was taken from the belly of a 300-pound pig at an Oregon

City meatpacking plant. The museums' collections also include two taxidermied eight-legged claves, a two-headed cow and a number of other stuffed animals. There are also Native American artifacts and a wonderful collection of Russian Orthodox icons, but to get inside either museum, you first have to go to the seminary's library to find someone to get the keys and turn on the lights.

- The Kidd Toy Museum in Portland features 15,000 antique toy trains, banks, railroads and more. Some of them are 150 years old and worth thousands of dollars. There are also dolls and other children's collectables...all are under glass so little prying fingers can't touch.

- The 3D Center of Art and Photography in Portland is the only museum in the United States dedicated entirely to antique and contemporary three-dimensional imagery. Some of its collection even goes as far back as the Civil War! The museum offers classes so you can learn how to make your own 3-D images.

- Hart's Reptile World in Canby is a family-run museum that's been a haven for discarded and abandoned reptiles since 1978.

- The Peterson Rock Garden and Museum in Redmond includes four acres of small-scale reproductions of monuments such as Independence Hall and the Statue of Liberty. All of them are accurate down to the smallest detail, and every one of them is made of glass, agates, jasper, malachite, obsidian, petrified wood and more.

- The Jensen Arctic Museum at the Western Oregon University campus in Monmouth is the only museum on the west coast of the lower 48 states that is dedicated entirely to the display and interpretation of Arctic culture.

OREGON'S AWESOME! San Francisco isn't the only city that had electric trolleys and streetcars all over the place with clanging bells taking passengers to and fro. Portland once had them and so did Eugene and Salem. Heck, they were even found in Albany, Astoria, Medford and West Linn! And if you want to relive the experience of what public transportation used to be like, stop by the Oregon Electric Railway Museum in Brooks. The largest trolley museum in the Pacific Northwest includes a mile of track, a newly constructed car-barn and a diverse fleet of 23 electric trolleys, buses and streetcars from around the world.

Historic Hanger

The world's largest wooden clear-span building? That's Hanger B, located at the Tillamook Air Museum. The U.S. Navy built the hanger in 1942–43. It housed eight "K" series airships during the war with its smaller companion, Hanger A, which burned down in 1992. These airships, or blimps as they are popularly called, carried eight to 10 men, four depth charges and two 50-caliber machine guns. With a 2000-mile range and the ability to stay aloft for three days, they searched for enemy submarines off the West Coast from San Francisco to the Straits of Juan de Fuca and engaged in convoy escort and air-sea rescue operations.

Hanger B is more than 15 stories tall, 296 feet wide and 1072 feet long. It covers more than seven acres. That's bigger than six football fields! The main doors are each 120 feet high.

Unfortunately, there are no blimps there today, but the museum does have a small fleet of planes and helicopters for those who are interested in aviation history. It includes a Corsair, a Mig, a Mustang, a Messerschmidt, a B-25, a Spitfire and a rare Japanese Nakajima Ki-43 Hayabusa. There's also an A4 Skyhawk simulator for those who want to find out what it's like to fly a jet!

Historical Legacy

There are plenty of museums for people who want to experience Oregon's history.

- Outside the Grant County Historical Museum in Canyon City are the famous poet Joaquin Miller's log cabin and the town of Greenhorn's one-room jail. Inside the museum are life-sized mannequins of early Native Americans who lived nearby and the miners who made Canyon City the most populated city in the state during the gold rush. The skulls of the first two men hanged in Canyon City and an assortment of two-headed bovines are also on display.

- Located in John Day, the Kam Wah Chung State Heritage Site is a museum dedicated to the memory of the Chinese contribution to Oregon's history. It's located in a building constructed in the 1860s where Dr. Ing Hay, an herbalist, practiced traditional medicine among gold mine workers and pioneers of the area. Along with thousands of artifacts of the time, the site is home to other period buildings including a pharmacy, general store and Chinese temple.

- Another legacy of Oregon's Chinese community are the 70 miles of tunnels that were built underneath Pendleton between 1870 and 1930. Entire businesses were located in those tunnels, including ice plants, butcher shops and laundries as well as saloons, bordellos and opium dens. Some of the tunnels have been restored and filled with exhibits. Once a year, live actors portray gamblers, merchants, musicians, dancers and all the other characters that used to live underground.

DID YOU  KNOW?

Founded in 1892, the Portland Art Museum is the oldest art museum in the Pacific Northwest and, with over 35,000 works of art, it's one of the largest in the country.

Scientifically Inclined
The Oregon Museum of Science and Industry is one of America's top 10 science museums. Its exhibits include the famed USS *Blueback* (the navy's last non-nuclear submarine, which was featured in the movie *The Hunt for Red October*) and the largest planetarium in the Pacific Northwest.

The High (Desert) Life

Bend's High Desert Museum contains Oregon's only desert-arium. In addition, the building, which houses 53,000 square feet of exhibits, is surrounded by acres of paved outdoor trails, allowing visitors to walk past live animal exhibits that include otters, foxes, wild cats and birds of prey. There's also a 19th-century homestead, a Native American camp, sawmill and mustang corral with actors portraying historic stagecoach drivers, mustang handlers, early settlers and more. There are even special events where you can participate in such activities as learning how to cook high-desert cuisine and view unique high-desert art.

MUSEUMS AND FESTIVALS

FUN IN THE SUN

A Fistful of Festivities
Every year, there are over 600 fairs, festivals and similar events across Oregon. That's almost two a day!

Welcome to the City of Roses
Portland—a.k.a. the Rose City—has been holding an annual Rose Festival since 1907. The 11-day event is held every June and attracts more than half a million guests each year. It offers the largest floral parade in the country as well as an illuminated Starlight Parade and a children's parade where kids and their parents can join the march! There's the Waterfront Village in downtown Portland where entertainment, food and thrill rides await one and all. American and Canadian naval ships dock along the Tom McCall Waterfront Park and open their decks to public tours. There's also the Rose Cup Race (the oldest amateur road race west of the Mississippi), a Grand Prix auto race, dragon boat races, a 3.1-mile run, fireworks and more! No wonder it is Portland's biggest civic event.

The Portland Saturday Market
The Portland Saturday Market is the largest continually operating open-air craft and farmers' market in the country. Open every Saturday and Sunday from March to December, over 400 vendors sell their baked goods, arts and crafts to the more than three quarters of a million visitors every year come to browse and to watch the street musicians, jugglers and dancers.

Eugene Market

The Portland Saturday Market may be the largest market of its kind in the country, but Eugene's Saturday Market, founded in 1970, is the oldest. Three hundred vendors sell their wares there every Saturday from April to November while live musicians and other performers entertain the customers.

Farmers Market

The Rose City is also host to the Portland Farmers' Market where, every April through December at four locations across town, over 250 farmers, bakers, butchers, fishermen, nurseries and others sell their wares to 22,000 customers every week.

Native American Pageantry

Every April, an estimated 1000 Umatilla, Warm Springs and Yakama Native Americans, as well as members of the general public, celebrate the return of the spring Chinook at the three-day Celilo Wyam First Salmon Feast and Pow-Wow in Celilo Village. Salmon, deer, elk, berries and roots are served to the sound of dancing, drumming and storytelling. The feast is accompanied by a day of ritual and prayer. According to tradition, the Native Americans' season for fishing and hunting cannot begin until the feast ends.

The Happy Canyon Pageant in Pendleton is proud to be one of the largest pow-wows around! Every September, 500 volunteer actors take three days to portray the life and cultures of early Native Americans, Lewis and Clark, Oregon Trail pioneers and typical residents of a frontier town. Fights break out, a bank is robbed, a couple falls in love and a square dance is held…on horseback! There's also gambling as well as two dances where the guests can kick up their feet and have fun.

Pig Races

Every one of Oregon's county fairs is a delight to attend, but only at the one in Tillamook County will you find the famous Pig-n-Ford Race! Held every August in Tillamook, the race begins with two days of qualifying rounds followed by the world championships on the third day.

The rules?

Step one: Contestants run to a pen on the opposite side of the racetrack and catch a live, squirming pig.

Step two: With the pig wedged firmly under one arm, contestants use a hand crank to start an 80-plus-year-old Model T.

Step three: Car started, each contestant gets inside his or her car—with the pig, of course—and makes a lap around the racetrack.

Step four: They stop their cars, turn off the engine and return the pigs to their pen. The first person to do this three times wins!

Oompah!
Mt. Angel's Oktoberfest is the oldest Oktoberfest and the largest folk festival in the Pacific Northwest. For four days in September, thousands converge upon the community to enjoy Bavarian cuisine, dancing, music, yodeling contests and, of course, a Biergarten and a Weingarten.

Life Aquatic

The Oregon Eel Fest is held every June in Oregon City and West Linn. Eel is not one the many food items served, but salmon and chicken are! There is a "Squiggle Ball" for those who like to dance and "Eel Tales" for those who like to hear great fish stories.

Staying Long in Pendleton?

The Pendleton Roundup is held in conjunction with the Happy Canyon Pageant and is regarded by many as the best rodeo in the country. There's bull riding, calf roping and steer wrestling competitions as well as a parade, cowboy breakfasts and country music concerts. During the seven-day event, Pendleton's population explodes from 15,000 to over 45,000!

You Don't Have to Leave the Willamette Valley to See a Rodeo

Every Fourth of July holiday weekend is the Molalla Buckaroo Rodeo. One of the largest and oldest rodeos in the state, there's even a carnival that goes with it as well as golf tournament, a Bar-B-Q contest, one of the largest Fourth of July parades in the state and fireworks (followed by live music and a dance).

Other Oregon Festival Facts

☛ The three-day Oregon Country Fair in Veneta, which stresses environmental awareness, naturalism and the nourishment of the spirit, requires crafts sold by vendors to be handmade and forbids the 50 food booths to serve anything created from processed ingredients.

☛ Over 250 pounds of bear meat and more than 250 fried rattlesnakes are served every September at the Canyon Day Bear and Rattlesnake Feed in Imnaha. There is also barrel racing, goat-tail tying and other activities. The event raises money for the school's scholarship fund.

☛ Sixteen tons of hot, buttered corn on the cob are served every August at the Aumsville Corn Festival! Another four tons are consumed a month later at the Founder's Day Corn Roast in Forest Grove.

☛ The world's largest strawberry shortcake is served every June for free to over 15,000 people at the Lebanon Strawberry Festival. The cake weighs 5700 pounds!

☛ Every year in February, just before St. Valentine's Day, the World Forestry Center in Portland holds a ChocolateFest for those who wish to sample, taste and learn about the delectable treat.

☛ Paisley brags of having a Mosquito Festival on the last weekend of every July. The town is home to some of the largest mosquitoes in the state and proceeds raised at the festival are used to control the pest.

☛ Get out the Old Blarney and shamrocks and join in on Lakeview's Irish Days. The annual March event is complete with a parade presided over by the Grand Leprechaun as well as potato-stick races and cow-chip flings.

MUSEUMS AND FESTIVALS

☛ July is the time for Lakeview's annual Hang Gliding Festival. It's no wonder Lakeview is called the Hang Gliding Capital of the West.

☛ North Plains has its Elephant Garlic Festival every August. Besides arts, crafts, food and music, there is also a Smelly King and Queen. (Anyone up for those jobs?)

☛ Lincoln City—home to three annual kite festivals—has been named one of the world's best places to fly kites by *Kitelines Magazine*.

YE OLDE FAIRES!

Come And Be Merry!

For two days every September at the Shrewsbury Renaissance Faire in Kings Valley, 24,000 Oregonians travel back 500 years to the time of Queen Elizabeth I and William Shakespeare. Jousting knights charge each other on a tournament field amid the shouts and applause of admiring fans. Minstrels, troubadours, dancers and bards entertain while 125 vendors sell unique handmade items and delicious treats. Over 1000 people working at the fair (and some of the public) appear in period costumes from England, Europe and the Middle East. Interactive living history displays and more are also available. The fair is the only one of its kind in Oregon.

Where Art Thou Romeo?

The Tony Award–winning Oregon Shakespeare Festival in Ashland is the largest repertory theater in the country and runs every February to October. Since it opened in 1935, the festival has staged Shakespeare's entire canon three times and has sold over 10 million tickets. Eleven plays, including an assortment of other playwrights' works, are performed each year at the festival's one outdoor and two indoor stages.

DID YOU  KNOW?

When the Oregon Shakespeare Festival first opened in 1935, it presented only one night's performance of *The Merchant of Venice* and two nights of *Twelfth Night*. Tickets cost 50 cents for adults and a quarter for children. Reserved seating was $1. The sponsors, afraid the theater wouldn't attract enough interest, insisted that boxing matches be held before the performances to draw in the crowds. But they had it all wrong: the plays made money and covered the losses from poor tickets sales for the boxing!

Moonlighting Actors
Famous actors who have performed at the Oregon Shakespeare Festival:

- William Hurt (*Kiss of the Spider Woman*)
- George Peppard (*Breakfast at Tiffany's*, *The A-Team*)
- Stacy Keach (*Mike Hammer*)
- Jean Smart (*Designing Women*)

Harry Anderson, famous for his role in *Night Court*, was once a live performer at the Green Show that is held before every evening's play.

Shakespeare's Ghost

Oscar-winner Charles Laughton (*The Private Life of Henry VIII*, *Mutiny on the Bounty*) was an accomplished Shakespearean stage actor who desperately wanted to perform at the Oregon Shakespeare Festival. In 1963, though seriously ill with cancer, Laughton was cast as King Lear. Unfortunately, he died in Hollywood on December 15, 1962, while practicing his lines. On the play's opening night in 1963, a cold wind suddenly blew off the hats of all the actors! Ever since, people believe that his ghost haunts the Elizabethan stage at the Shakespeare Festival and claim to hear low, eerie moans during performances of *King Lear*.

MUSIC FESTIVALS

Some of Oregon's great music festivals:

- Every July in Eugene, over 32,000 people listen to world-class musicians and singers perform the composer's works at the two-week Oregon Bach Festival.

- At the Mount Angel Abbey's annual three-day Abbey Bach Festival, you'll hear Vespers sung by a group of Benedictine monks, enjoy a large picnic and then listen to a full-length evening concert.

- The largest blues festival west of the Mississippi (and the second largest in the country) is Portland's five-day Safeway Waterfront Blues Festival. Over 125 musicians perform, and all proceeds go to the Oregon Food Bank.

- Shaniko's Ragtime and Vintage Music Festival takes place in "Oregon's Best Known Ghost Town."

- Classical, pop, country, bluegrass, blues, folk and jazz music is performed under beautiful ponderosa pines and Madrona evergreens in a naturally formed amphitheater every June through September at the Britt Festival in Jacksonville.

PORTLAND

THE CITY OF ROSES

Portland has been known as the "City of Roses" for over 100 years. The name was first applied in 1888 by tourists who were attending an Episcopal Church convention in the city. The Portland Rose Society was formed that same year, and 1889 saw Portland's first annual rose show. By 1905, the city had 20 miles of streets with the fragrant flower planted along their sidewalks. In 1907, Portland presented its first Rose Festival, an annual event that now attracts over half a million people every year.

Today, Portland has many rose gardens, but the most famous is the four and a half acre International Rose Test Garden which houses over 10,000 rose plants and more than 500 varieties of the flower. Newly cultivated roses from around the world are sent to the garden to be tested for their color, fragrance and resistance to disease.

DID YOU  KNOW?

The International Rose Test Garden was originally a refuge for European hybrid roses. The garden was created in 1917 at the height of the World War I because of fears that the fighting and devastation in Europe would destroy all of the unique plants. It is the oldest continuously operating public rose test garden in the country.

A Rose By Any Other Name

The City of Roses has also been called Stumptown because of all the tree stumps left behind by logging in the city's early days and Puddletown because of all the rain!

DID YOU  KNOW?

Portland's Classical Chinese Garden is the largest urban suzhou-style garden outside China.

The Oregon Zoo

The Oregon Zoo in Portland cares for more than 200 species of animals. Twenty-one of them are endangered species and 33 are threatened. With over 1.3 million visitors a year, it is the most popular fee-charging attraction in the state. What few of these visitors realize, however, is that the zoo started in the back of a drugstore!

Drugstore Zoo
In the 1870s, Richard Knight, a Portland seaman-turned-pharmacist, began to collect animals from around the world that his former shipmates gave to him when they visited. His collection included small exotic animals and birds, and he kept them in the back of his store. But when he acquired two nine-foot-tall, 800-pound bears, they needed a new home! He tried to sell the bears to the city in 1888, but he was only given permission to house them in circus cages at what is now Washington Park. At the end of the year, Knight approached the city again, but this time to donate one of the bears. The city accepted the offer, and the first zoo west of the Mississippi River was created.

When Packy the Asian elephant was born at the Oregon Zoo on April 14, 1962, he was the first elephant born in the Western Hemisphere in 44 years. Today, Packy's still making history! At 13,870 pounds and 10 feet 6 inches at the shoulder, he is the largest Asian elephant in the United States. Since his birth, 27 more elephant calves (including Packy's seven kids) have been born at the Oregon Zoo, making it the most successful zoo elephant-breeding program in the world!

A First Among Zoos!
From the very beginning, the Oregon Zoo was making zoological history! The original site included the world's first sunken, barless cage for bears.

The Oregon Zoo was originally called the Portland Zoological Gardens. It changed its name to the Washington Park Zoo in 1976 and got its current name in 1998.

Kids and Trees

Next door to the Oregon Zoo are the World Forestry Center and the Portland Children's Museum. Established in 1949, the Children's Museum was one of the first of its kind. With its story-tellers, puppeteers and dancers as well and a market where the kiddies can shop for the family's dinner, everyone in the family will have a good time.

The World Forestry Center has 20,000 square feet of exhibits and displays as well as two working forests devoted to teaching young and old about the world's trees and their importance to all life on the planet.

Let's Go See a Movie!

Per capita, Portland has more movie theaters than any other city in the country. There are over 50 of them within 20 miles of the downtown core. Believe it or not, that's down from the 70 that were in the Rose City in 1915!

These theaters include a number of independents that show classics, second-run movies and independent and foreign films. There are even "brew-n-view" theaters, where patrons watch the movie from couches and comfy chairs while enjoying a cold beer. The city is also host to a large number of film festivals that celebrate international, gay and lesbian, Jewish, underground, environmental, documentary and experimental movies.

Portland Potpourri

☛ Portland's residents drink more gourmet coffee per capita than those of any other city in the United States.

☛ More people per capita bike to work in Portland than any other city in the United States. And no wonder: there are 160 miles of bike lanes, 70 miles of off-street paths and 30 miles of "bike boulevards" where automobile traffic is limited! There are also bike-parking facilities all across the city.

- In 2006, Portland ranked first in the American Podiatric Medical Association's list of best cities for walking. Makes sense when you reflect on all the walking clubs and free walking events in the city. The annual Portland Marathon has also been voted the country's "most friendly walkers marathon."

- Portland also has more miles of rail transit, per capita, than any other major city in the nation.

- Portland has more bookstores per capita than any other city in the United States. It also ranks second for the number of books sold.

- Every year, over 19 million items are checked out of the Multnomah County's 14 branch libraries. That's the largest circulation of any public library system in the United States. And according to Hennen's American Public Library Ratings, it's the second best library serving a city of more than 500,000 people in the country.

- Portland has more microbreweries and brewpubs per capita than any other American city. It's also ranked fifth for the most bars and taverns per capita in the United States.

- Portland has more strip clubs per capita than any other city in the United States. As of 2005, Seattle had four, San Francisco 17, Las Vegas 30 and Portland 41 (though some sources put the number at over 50!).

Commuters!

Not every Portlander works in Multnomah County. In 2000, 10 percent of the city's residents commuted to Washington County to work, eight percent to Clackamas County and two percent to Clark County, Washington.

Likewise, not everyone who works in Multnomah County is local. An astounding 34 percent of Clackamas County's residents who had jobs in 2000 worked in Multnomah County. And the same is true for large segments of the working populations of Columbia County, Washington County and Yamhill County and Clark County, Washington.

DID YOU  KNOW?

The median income of Portland residents in 2004 was $41,128 per year. That makes Stumptown 28th on the list of America's most prosperous cities.

Giant Woman
The second largest hammered copper statue in the United States is *Portlandia*, a 36-foot-high, 6.5-ton copper statue of a giant kneeling woman in classical garb with a trident in her right hand who stares down at pedestrians from the third floor of the Portland Building. Inspired by the woman on Portland's official seal, she'd be 50 feet tall if she was standing. Only the Statue of Liberty is bigger. But don't worry; while Portlandia is holding the trident in one hand, she's reaching out her other to greet you.

Want to Have a Baby?
Portland was named in February 2007 by *Fit Pregnancy* magazine as the fourth best city in the country to have a child. Only Boston, San Francisco and Minneapolis were ranked higher.

Oscar's Official Chocolates
Portland's Moonstruck Chocolate Company was the official provider of the chocolates that went into the gift baskets at the 2006 and 2007 Academy Awards ceremonies. And we're not just talking about chocolate-covered cashews here, but rare arriba from Ecuador, chuao from Venezuela, mangaro from Madagascar and much more.

Have a Sweet Tooth?

Tanea Whittaker has devoted years to make the house from where she runs her Keana's Candyland candy and catering business look as if it's made from real candy. On the outside, hundreds of candy canes, candy corn, cookies, lollipops and starlight mints have been placed on top of bricks covered with white grout. Inside, chandeliers look like cupcakes and ice cream sodas, and the walls are all painted according the theme of the room. One room is decorated with beautiful murals of castles, fairylands and flying horses. Unfortunately, most of the delicious-looking goodies on the walls are inedible, but the gourmet chocolates and pastries that Tanea makes are certainly tasty!

Other Giant Portland Attractions

☛ A 35-foot tall Paul Bunyan statue greets visitors entering from the north side of Portland on Interstate 5 in the city's Kenton neighborhood. Located at the corner of North Interstate and North Denver, it was built for the Oregon Centennial celebrations that were held in Kenton in 1959.

☛ And a 16-foot-tall bronze He-man, which was once an outdoor roadside attraction, now greets visitors to Giant's Gym at 52nd and Sandy. The statue sits in the middle of the gym's weight room and is so tall that he pokes through a hole in the gym's drop ceiling.

Powell's Books' 74,000-square-foot flagship store takes up an entire city block. It offers more than one million books and 40,000 DVDs for purchase in person, by phone or via the company's website. Each year, the family-owned store and its six satellite locations sell over four million books. That's 3000 to 5000 every day, and that doesn't include the 1000 books it sells each day over the Internet! Believe it or not, even Amazon.com orders thousands of out-of-print books from Powell's every year. *Internet Retailer Magazine* included Powell's Books on its list of the country's top 50 online retailers in 2005. The bookstore is open 365 days a year and people have even been married there!

The Powell's Books store on Burnside has almost 250 sections from art (which alone has 149 subsections) to world history. There's even a section for banned books!

Powell's Pillar

Installed in 2000 at the northwest entrance of Powell's Burnside location is a nine-foot-tall sandstone pillar. On its base are Latin inscriptions that translate roughly "buy the book," "read the book," "enjoy the book" and "sell the book." Eight 500-pound stone books with titles such as *Hamlet* and *The Odyssey* sit atop this base.

DID YOU  KNOW?

In 2006, *Portland Mercury* readers ranked local businesses by the sexiness of their staff. Powell's staff was named the second sexiest in Portland! The bookstore was also the only establishment on the list whose main line of business isn't serving booze or food.

Oregon's Largest Shopping Mall

That's Lloyd Center in Portland. When it opened in 1960, it was the largest urban shopping mall in the country; some claimed that it was the largest in the world. It may have lost these titles, but with only a bit less than 1.5 million square feet of office and retail space, a 900-seat food court, 18 movie theaters and an indoor ice-skating rink, Lloyd Center is still the biggest shopping center in Oregon.

Let's Go to The Oaks!

The Oaks Amusement Park opened in 1905 and is the oldest continuously operating amusement park in the country. Its historic carousel was built in 1912, and its wooden roller-skating rink, complete with a Wurlitzer pipe organ, is the largest on the West Coast.

EAT, DRINK AND BE MERRY

World's Smallest Restaurant

Briggs and Crampton Caterer's Table for Two has only one table, which seats only two people. The restaurant is open for lunch Tuesday through Friday, but only one lucky couple is served per day. There is no set menu and customers don't know what they'll eat until they get there. These gourmet meals have been known to last up to five hours!

Portland's Oldest Restaurant and Bar

Huber's has been serving turkey dinners and flaming Spanish coffees since 1879. In fact, it sells so many of these delicious drinks that it uses more Kahlúa than any other bar or restaurant in the country!

A Voodoo "I Do" with Doughnuts

Voodoo Doughnut is famous for its tasty doughnuts. Anyone ready for another Triple Chocolate Penetration or a Grape Ape? But the owners are also ordained ministers of the Universal Life Church Monastery and perform legally valid marriages at their shop. For $175, you can get married under Voodoo's doughnut-shaped Cruller Chandelier of Life and a velvet painting of Isaac Hayes. Doughnuts and coffee for 10 are included in the fee. Free Swahili lessons are also taught at Voodoo every Monday night, and there's a doughnut-eating contest every month. Several of Portland's budding bands and actors have performed there for the customers.

Oregon Beer

Oregon has more breweries per capita than any other state, and in 1990, Portland was proclaimed "America's Microbrew Capital." There's a good reason.

Mass-produced lagers are often made with malt from corn and rice, little compressed hop-dust pellets and water from chlorinated municipal water supplies. In Oregon, farmers grow fine grains such as barley and wheat and dozens of varieties of heirloom hops, all of which are near at hand for the state's 60 or more craft breweries. Throw Oregon's famously fresh, naturally pure water into the mix, and the state's master brewers are able to offer a wide variety of beers certain to please even the most discerning palate.

Want to Sample a Brew?
The Spring Beer and Wine Fest is held in Portland every April. It's the largest springtime brew-sampling event in the United States. And don't forget its cousin, the Oregon Brewers Festival, a four-day event that attracts over 55,000 people every July. It's considered to be one of the best craft beer festivals in the country.

Some Frothy Firstx

- America's first craft beer quality-assurance program was introduced by the Oregon Brewers Guild in 1998.
- The Roots Brewing Company was Oregon's first all-organic brewery. It opened in Portland in 2005.
- The country's first employee-owned brewery was the Full Sail Brewery of Hood River. In business since 1987, it became employee-owned 12 years later.

July is Oregon Craft Beer Month.

But Don't Get the Wrong Idea...

Despite all the craft brews, Portlanders aren't snobs when it comes to beer. They drink more Pabst Blue Ribbon than anyone else in America!

A Night at the Symphony

Portland's first symphonic music concert was held in 1866 at the Oro Fino Hall. Thirty years later, the Portland Symphony Society was created. It was the first symphony orchestra in the western United States. It was renamed the Oregon Symphony in 1967, and it is the sixth oldest orchestra in the country.

Established in 1924, the Portland Youth Philharmonic, which consists of 260 students between the ages of seven and 22, is the oldest youth orchestra in the United States.

Outstanding Opera
The Portland Opera Company is ranked among the top 15 opera companies in North America.

A Storied Hall

The Portland Symphony Society's Arlene Schnitzer Concert Hall used to be a 3000-seat movie theater. Opened in 1928 for vaudeville acts, it became the Paramount Theater two years later and showed movies until 1972.

In its early years, the "Schnitz" was the largest and most lavish movie theater of any similarly sized city in the United States. It had the longest candy counter west of the Mississippi as well as antique furniture, original oil paintings, three grand pianos, a pipe organ, velvet drapes, Oriental rugs and a 16th-century suit of armor.

A Different Kind of Show
That's Mary's Club in Portland—the oldest strip club in Oregon. Originally a piano club where merchant seamen could eat and drink while being entertained with music, topless go-go dancers were introduced in 1965 only as a way to keep the customers from leaving whenever the piano players took a break. The girls soon became more popular than the musicians, and out the piano players went. All-nude dancing came 20 years later.

PORTLAND PARKS

Portland's first park was established in 1852, only one year after the city was incorporated. Today, Portland has more than 250 city parks that cover over 10,000 acres and ranks ninth among the large cities in the United States in terms of the percentage of land within its boundaries that is devoted to parks—almost 16 percent.

The Smallest Park
Mills End Park is a two-foot diameter circle at the intersection of SW Naito and SW Taylor in downtown Portland. A mere 452 square inches, it is the smallest park in the world. Founded on St. Patrick's Day in 1948 by newspaper columnist Dick Fagan as a park for leprechauns and snail races, it has sported a swimming pool for butterflies (complete with diving board) and a miniature Ferris wheel. It made it into the *Guinness Book of Records* in 1971 and became an official city park in 1976.

The Largest Park
Established in 1948 on the hillsides overlooking the Willamette River, Portland's 5156-acre Forest Park is home to more than 100 types of birds and over 60 species of animals. The park also includes over 70 miles of recreational trails, a massive tree canopy and substantial undergrowth. It is the largest naturally forested area within the city limits of any municipality in America and the third largest city park of any kind in the country.

Down With Roads!
Portland is the only major city in the United States to dismantle a downtown expressway in order to create a park. Harbor Drive was torn apart between 1974 and 1978 and replaced with the 36.6-acre Tom McCall Waterfront Park.

Not Quite a Park...

From 1850 to 1941, Portland was known as the "Shanghai Capital of the World" because so many people were kidnapped in the city! A network of tunnels underneath the city's waterfront connected many of the city's pool halls, saloons, restaurants, brothels, gambling parlors and opium dens. Unsuspecting men and women—as many as 1500 per year!—were drugged, dropped into the tunnels and then sold for $50 to $55 as prostitutes or ships' crewmembers.

The trapdoors, secret entrances and tunnels remain, and more tunnels are discovered all the time. The Cascade Geographic Society gives tours for the curious.

CITY TRIVIA

FACTS AND FIGURES

There are 240 incorporated cities in Oregon. Only 42 of them have populations greater than 10,000. Nearly 100 have less than 1000 residents. Six that have populations of less than 100!

In Oregon, incorporated cities have a formally organized government with a mayor and city council. They may also levy taxes to provide services such as police, libraries, parks and sanitation. To incorporate a new city, at least 150 people must live within the proposed city limits, and no territory belonging to another city may be included in the proposed borders. If enough residents sign a petition calling for incorporation, an election will be held. If the vote is favorable, then Oregon has a new city!

Of course, most cities are established long before they are formally incorporated, and today, there are many unincorporated communities across the state, including a few with populations of over 10,000.

Cities, Towns and Hamlets

The first city to be incorporated in the state was Oregon City in 1844. The most recent was La Pine. Although founded in 1910, residents only incorporated their community in 2006. The same year, voters in Bull Mountain rejected a proposal to incorporate.

In 1976, the city of Juntura voted 29 to 1 to disincorporate.

Towns are mentioned in the state constitution, but there is no provision for creating one in Oregon's laws.

Clackamas County recently decided to allow residents to create villages and hamlets. These municipalities have some of the powers and responsibilities of incorporated cities but no paid staff.

In 2006, the residents of Brightwood, Rhododendron, Welches, Wemme and Zigzag voted to become the Villages of Mount Hood. They are the first—and only—village in the state.

There are presently only two hamlets: Beavercreek and Stafford.

Oregon's 10 Biggest Cities

City	Population: 2000	Est. Population 2006	% Increase
Portland	529,121	562,690	6.3
Salem	136,924	149,305	9.0
Eugene	137,893	148,595	7.8
Gresham	90,205	97,745	8.4
Hillsboro	70,186	84,445	20.3
Beaverton	76,129	84,270	10.7
Bend	52,029	75,290	44.7
Medford	63,154	73,960	17.1
Springfield	52,864	57,065	8.0
Corvallis	49,322	53,900	9.3

DID YOU  KNOW?

Sheridan is Oregon's fastest growing city. It had only 3570 residents in 2000, but grew to an estimated 5785 in 2006. That's a 62 percent increase in only six years!

Mega-Cities

City population figures hide the fact that many communities close to each other have grown to the point that they've really merged into mega-cities. Without looking for the street signs, who can tell when you've left Portland and entered Gresham, Lake Oswego, Oak Grove or Tigard?

According to the 2000 census, there are 1,298,697 people living in the Portland urban area. There are 224,049 in Eugene's urban area; 207,229 in Salem's; and 128,780 in Medford's.

Even though 34.3 percent of the state's population live in cities of less than 2500 or in communities that are not incorporated, that doesn't mean they all live a rural life. All of the major cities have highly populated, but unincorporated, areas near their city limits. In fact, according to the U.S. Census Bureau, only 21.3 percent of Oregonians were living in rural areas in 2000.

Oregon Cities: Great Places to Live!
In 2006, *Men's Journal* magazine named Portland the best place to live in the United States. (Austin, Texas, and Boulder, Colorado, were second and third.) It named Hood River the American city offering the highest quality of living while also allowing people to be physically active and healthy. Eugene was among the best cities for singles to meet, and the small town of Bonanza was one of the best destinations for people wanting to get away from big city life.

FUN CITY FACTS

There She Blows! (In More Ways Than One)
Florence acquired international fame in 1970 as the city that exploded a whale. When an eight-ton sperm whale beached itself near Florence and died, the tides weren't strong enough to pull it out to sea. Fearing that, if buried, the carcass would be uncovered by the waves, state officials, in consultation with the U.S. Navy, decided to blow the whale into little pieces that birds and bugs would carry off.

A half-ton of dynamite was carefully placed, but rather than reducing the corpse to tiny pieces, the resulting explosion simply hurled large chunks of whale blubber far into the air. When they came down, one smashed a car. Most of the body remained intact and had to be hauled away.

The event was caught on film and broadcast around the world. More recently, footage of the explosion has found its way to the Internet. As a result, nearly 40 years after the event, state officials still get calls about the explosion. They even have to field complaints about animal abuse from people who don't realize the whale was already dead when they blew it up!

Today, when a whale beaches itself, the body is either burned and then buried on the beach or towed out to open sea.

Astoria

One hundred years ago, Astoria was the second largest city in Oregon. But today, it is a relatively small community best known as a tourist destination, a center for the arts and a filming location. (It's provided the backdrop for no fewer than nine Hollywood movies, including *The Ring* and both episodes of *Free Willy*.) The city's downtown has been razed twice by fire, once in 1883 and again in 1922, but was resilient enough to rebuild each time.

CITY TRIVIA

A Famous Capitalist

Astoria was named after John Jacob Astor, America's first millionaire. He made his money from the fur trade and real estate and would be worth billions today. In 1811, one of his companies established Fort Astoria, the first permanent American settlement on the Pacific Coast.

DID YOU KNOW?

John Jacob Astor's great-grandson, John Jacob Astor IV, was the richest man on the *Titanic* when it sank in 1912. At the time, he was worth about $200 million. Astor personally helped his five-month-pregnant wife into a lifeboat. Supposedly, as the ship was sinking, Astor complained, "I asked for ice, but this is ridiculous."

City of Ballast

Much of downtown Astoria sits on boulders that were used as ballast by the ships that came into Youngs Bay. The shoreline was originally where Exchange Street is today.

A Mighty Long Bridge

The world's longest continuous truss-span bridge links Astoria, Oregon, to Megler, Washington. It crosses the mouth of the Columbia River and is 4.21 miles long! Ships can sail under the 200-foot-tall arch on the Oregon side, but the two miles leading into Washington are only 25 feet above sea level. Opened in 1966, after four years and at a cost of $24 million, there was initially a $1.50 toll, but it was dropped in 1994 when, two years ahead of schedule, the bridge was paid for with the funds that were raised. Before the bridge was completed, folks trying to cross the river had to take a ferry.

Only Column of Its Kind
The Astoria Column is 125 feet high and depicts 14 scenes from Astoria's history. A 164-step staircase inside the column leads to a platform offering spectacular views of the Pacific, the Columbia River, Youngs Bay and various lakes and mountains. And watch out for falling debris! School children and tourists often throw small balsawood planes bought from the local gift shop off the top of the column to see how far they will go.

DID YOU  KNOW?

The Astoria Column is built on the 600-foot Coxcomb Hill, which was the site of the first permanent American settlement west of the Rocky Mountains.

A Little Bit of Italy
The column's design is patterned after the ancient Trajan's Column in Rome, Italy.

That's Some House!
The Rose House in Oregon City is perhaps the most important residence in the state's political history. Built in 1847 by William and Louisa Holmes, the home was the place where Oregon was declared a United States territory in 1849. That same year, Oregon's territorial legislature met there for the first time. Joseph Lane gave his inaugural address as Oregon's first territorial governor from the second floor balcony. The house is now a museum.

A Revolutionary War Veteran
William Cannon, the only soldier from the American Revolution buried in Oregon, arrived in the state in 1811 as an employee of John Jacob Astor's American Fur Company and never left. A private with the Fourth Pennsylvania Artillery during the war, he died in 1854 at the age of 99 and is buried at St. Paul.

CITY TRIVIA

OREGON'S AWESOME! According to the book *Retirement Places Rated*, Florence is the number one spot in the entire country for retirees to live. The rating was based on such factors as climate, cost of living, cultural and recreational activities and general ambiance. Apparently the word has been out for some time—38.2 percent of the city's population is at least 65 years old, and the median age of its residents is 55.8 years!

Brave Lads

Pacific City is a nice, small fishing community and vacation spot on the coast that doesn't have a single wharf, dock or pier! Since the early 1900s, fishermen have launched their dories directly from the beach at Cape Kiwanda to challenge the breakers as they head out to sea to fish for salmon. In the old days, the dories were powered only by oars and the strength of their crew's arms, but modern outboard motors now allow them to go as far as 50 miles from shore. In the 1960s and '70s, the double-ended fishing boats in Oregon's only dory fleet numbered in the hundreds, but because of competition from larger commercial fishing vessels, there are only a few left today.

CITY TRIVIA

More Quick Fun

- Thousands of people mail their Christmas cards from the post office at Christmas Valley. Upon request, they can even have them canceled by hand on December 24 or 25.

- North Bend is actually about 45 miles south (and 150 miles west) of Bend.

- Lincoln City is on the 45th parallel—that's exactly halfway between the Equator and the North Pole!

- The entire city of Jacksonville was designated a National Historic Landmark in 1966. It was the first national historic landmark in Oregon.

- The Snowy Butte Mill, built in 1872 at Eagle Point, is the only gristmill still operating in Oregon.

- Summer Lake is a small town divided into two sections that are a mile apart—with nothing in between!

- Monmouth legalized the sale of alcohol in 2002. It was the last municipality in the western continental United States to practice prohibition.

- The largest wireless "wi-fi" network in the world operates out of Hermiston. It provides Internet service to a 700-square-mile area. Local officials even use it to check parking meters.

- Back in 1978, 49 three-inch cannonballs were found between Wagontire and Riley. No one knows where they came from or who left them there.

Four, Three, Two, One
Members of OregonRocketry meet in the miles of flat sagebrush covered terrain surrounding the community of Brothers four times a year to launch their model and high-power amateur

rockets. Some of them go tens of thousands of feet into the air! These rocket enthusiasts also meet twice a year at Sheridan.

San Francisco Hangs in Oregon City

For years, the original city plan for San Francisco hung on the wall of the county clerk's office at the Clackamas County Courthouse! Why? Well, in 1850, the only federal courthouse west of the Rockies was in Oregon City, so the plan had to be filed there. The plan is now on display at Oregon City's Museum of the Oregon Territory.

An Entire Town Moves

Arlington lies on the southern bank of the Columbia River where Interstate 84 and Highway 19 meet. But in 1963, the town had to move. Why? Most of its business area, as well as many homes, were on the flat lands that were going to be flooded as a result of the construction of the John Day Dam. So the town moved to the surrounding foothills from which residents now have a beautiful view of Lake Umatilla, the reservoir that was created behind the dam. And the original city? Buildings, streets and all are fully preserved in the chilly waters at the bottom of the 200-foot-deep lake.

Split Personalities?

Half of the community of New Pine Creek is in Oregon and the other half is in California. But it's not the only Oregon town with a split personality: both Denio and McDermitt straddle the Oregon–Nevada border.

There are advantages to this situation. McDermitt's White Horse Inn, which sits on the state line, used to serve meals on the Oregon side to avoid Nevada's sales tax and maintained a brothel on the Nevada side to avoid Oregon's vice squad!

COUNTY TRIVIA

JUST THE FACTS

Oregon has 36 counties. Listed alphabetically, they are:

Baker	Lake
Benton	Lane
Clackamas	Lincoln
Clatsop	Linn
Columbia	Malheur
Coos	Marion
Crook	Morrow
Curry	Multnomah
Deschutes	Polk
Douglas	Sherman
Gilliam	Tillamook
Grant	Umatilla
Harney	Union
Hood River	Wallowa
Jackson	Wasco
Jefferson	Washington
Josephine	Wheeler
Klamath	Yamhill

The Size Prize

Oregon's five largest counties in terms of square miles are:

Harney: 10,134
Malheur: 9887
Lake: 8136
Klamath: 5944
Douglas: 5036

DID YOU KNOW?

Harney County is bigger than Connecticut, Delaware, Hawaii, Maryland, Massachusetts, New Hampshire, New Jersey, Rhode Island and Vermont. That's nine states!

Small but Great
Not to be overlooked, Oregon's five smallest counties in terms of square miles are:

Multnomah: 435	Benton: 676
Hood River: 522	Yamhill: 716
Columbia: 656	

Most Populous Counties
Oregon's smallest county is also its most populated—over 675,000 Oregonians call Multnomah County home. In fact, more than half of the state's population lives in Multnomah, Washington, Clackamas, Lane and Marion counties.

Least Populated Counties
Some of Oregon's biggest counties are also among its least populated. The five counties with the fewest people are Wallowa, Harney, Gilliam, Sherman and Wheeler. The last three counties each have less than 2000 residents!

Like Crowds?
Let's face it. Some people like the hustle and bustle of the city, while others prefer the peace and quiet of the country. According to the 2000 census, an average of 35.6 people lived in every square mile of land in Oregon in 2000 compared to the national average of 79.6 people per square mile. The most densely populated county in Oregon is Multnomah County, with 1517.6 residents per square mile. The least densely populated was Harney County, with less than one resident per square mile!

Where Do You Want to Live (If You're a Duck or a Fish)?
Lake County is aptly named. Over 222 square miles of its area are covered by lakes, ponds, rivers and other bodies of water. But believe it or not, it's not the wettest county in Oregon!

Curry, Clatsop and Tillamook have even more land covered by water.

The Ghost County

Back in 1851, the sudden influx of miners necessitated the creation of Umpqua County in the southwest part of Oregon. The county government went back and forth between Elkton and Scottsburg before the territorial legislature finally settled on the former as the county seat in 1855. The county seat was later located at Green Valley and then at Yoncalla.

Umpqua county's boundaries almost immediately came under attack. In 1852, Douglas County was created out of the parts of Umpqua County east of the Coast Range. The following year, Lane County was created from Umpqua County's northern half, while Coos County (which then included present-day Curry County) took everything south of the Umpqua River. What was left was absorbed by Douglas County in 1863.

Umpqua is now often referred to as the Ghost County of Oregon.

CLAIMS TO FAME

Baker County
This county was once heralded as the largest gold producer in the northwest and contains the world's deepest gorge, Hells Canyon.

Crook County
Steins Pillar is a monolithic column in the Ochoco Mountains of Crook County and measures 400 feet in height and 120 feet in diameter. It wasn't scaled by rock climbers until 1950.

Curry County
Ninety percent of all Easter lilies grown in the United States are produced in Curry County.

Harney County
Harney's human population may be small, but it is home to over 100,000 head of cattle!

Hood River County
Hood River County produces more Anjou pears than any other place in the world.

Lake County
The world's oldest shoes—a pair of 9000-year-old bark sandals—were discovered in Lake County in 1938. Prior to the discovery, it was thought people had only been living in the Pacific Northwest for 4000 years.

Morrow County
Despite its 2000-plus square miles and 11,000 residents, Morrow County doesn't have a single traffic light.

Sherman County
Primarily a farming community occupying 831 square miles of land, the population of Sherman County has remained constant for the last 100 years. About 2000 people call it home.

Wasco County
When Wasco County was created in 1854, it covered 130,000 square miles! Its borders included all of Oregon east of the Cascades, the southern two-thirds of Idaho and portions of Montana and Wyoming. Since it was the first county established after the United States took sole possession of Oregon, it can be said that Wasco was the largest county ever formed in the country.

Wheeler County
Wheeler County is known worldwide for its large store of fossils. The county's archaeological and geological riches can be experienced firsthand at the 14,000-acre John Day Fossil Beds National Monument.

Yamhill County
In the middle of a Yamhill County farmer's field sits a 40-ton boulder that was scooped up during the last glacial ice age and deposited there about 20,000 years ago.

COUNTY TRIVIA

COUNTIES NAMED AFTER FAMOUS FOLKS

Honoring Past Presidents
Three Oregon counties were named for dead presidents.

Washington County was originally called the Twality District but was renamed in 1849 in honor of the father of our country, George Washington.

In 1852, Jackson County was created and named for Andrew Jackson, a.k.a. "Old Hickory."

Lincoln County was established in 1893 and was named for the Great Emancipator, Abraham Lincoln.

Jefferson County was only indirectly named for a dead president. It took its name from Mount Jefferson, a 10,495-foot mountain on the county's western border that is the second highest peak in the state. Mount Jefferson was named for President Thomas Jefferson in 1806 by the explorers Meriwether Lewis and William Clark who were then on their way back to Missouri after wintering near present-day Astoria.

One Living President
James K. Polk was very much alive and still in the White House when Polk County was created and named for him in 1845. The county seat, Dallas, was named after his vice president, George Dallas.

One Future President
When Grant County was named after Ulysses S. Grant in 1864, he hadn't been elected president yet! He was still the commander-in-chief of the United States Army and was busy fighting the Confederates in Virginia.

Commander of Oregon's First Army
In 1885, Gilliam County was named for Colonel Cornelius Gilliam, the commander of Oregon's first army during the Cayuse Indian War in 1847.

Politician Turned Soldier
Baker County was created in 1862 and named after Edward Dickinson Baker, a prominent lawyer, Illinois congressman, Mexican War veteran and close friend of Abraham Lincoln. Lincoln even named one of his sons after Baker. He served as one of Oregon's earliest United States senators before being killed as an officer in the Union Army early in the Civil War.

Missouri Statesmen
In 1847, Oregonians named two of their counties, Benton and Linn, after two United States senators from Missouri who advocated the westward expansion of the United States and the settlement of Oregon.

A Little Giant
Senator Stephen Douglas of Illinois was only five feet four inches tall and weighed a mere 90 pounds, but was a famously expressive speaker who objected to the division of Oregon with the British and helped establish Oregon's territorial government. In January 1852, state Democrats who supported Douglas' bid to become their presidential nominee named Douglas County in his honor.

Local Army Commander
In 1889, Harney County was named after William Shelby Harney, a career military officer who commanded the U.S. Army's Department of Oregon from 1858 to 1860. The county also has a Harney Lake and a Harney Valley.

Revolutionary War Hero

Originally called the Champooick District and then Champoeg County, Marion County was named after Revolutionary War General Francis Marion, a.k.a. the "Swamp Fox," in 1849. By the 1840s, Marion was a legendary hero to most Americans.

Early Oregon Politician

Lane County was named in 1851 after Joseph Lane, an Indiana legislator and Mexican War general who was appointed Oregon's first territorial governor in 1849. Lane also led the military campaign against the Rogue River tribe in 1851. He later became one of Oregon's first United States senators and ran for vice president in 1860.

Early Female Settler

Josephine County was named in 1856 for 23-year-old Josephine Rollins, the first white woman to settle in southern Oregon. Ironically, in 1856, Josephine was living in California with her husband Julius Ort.

Another General

Sherman County was created the same day as Harney County in 1889. Originally, it was going to be named after James Fulton, an early settler who struck it rich there. But Fulton was a fiercely partisan Democrat, and Republicans controlled the state legislature. The county was named after the Union general William Tecumseh Sherman instead.

After an Admiral

Hood River County was established in 1908 and named after the largest river and city within its borders. The river was named in the late 1850s after Mount Hood, which had been named years earlier in honor of British admiral Lord Samuel Hood. Hood fought against the Americans during the 1776 Revolution, which means that Hood River County is indirectly named after a British war hero!

A Stage Coach Driver?
Wheeler County was named in 1899 after Oregon's most famous stagecoach driver, Henry H. Wheeler.

In the early 1860s, gold brought thousands of miners to Canyon Creek, eventually making the newly formed Canyon City the largest city in the state! But with no passenger service to carry them the 180 dangerous miles to The Dalles, residents were cut off from the rest of the world. So Wheeler established the Dalles to Canyon City Stage Line in 1864.

A one-way trip took about two days and cost $40 (or about $600 in today's dollars). He drove three stages a week. Wheeler also delivered mail, and Wells Fargo hired him to run express coaches between The Dalles and Canyon City that carried only gold and guards.

Wheeler braved bandits, bullets and unfriendly Native Americans, and was shot once when his stage was attacked. He finally sold his stage line in 1868 and was still living in the area when the state named Wheeler County in his honor.

Indian Fighter

Crook County was named in 1882 for the U.S. Army's most successful Indian fighter, General George Crook.

A Young Oregon Politician

Curry County was named in 1855 for Oregon territorial governor George L. Curry. He was the first Oregonian to hold the post.

A River

Columbia County was named after the Columbia River. Captain Robert Gray had named the river after his ship, the *Columbia Rediviva*.

DID YOU  KNOW?

The *Columbia Rediviva* was the first American ship to circumnavigate the world. A full-scale replica has been sailing around Mark Twain's Island at Disneyland since 1956.

Pro-Northern Sympathies

When Union County was established in 1864, it was named after the city of Union located within its boundaries. That community was founded in 1862 and was named to reflect its residents' pro-northern sympathies during the Civil War.

Lakes Here, Lakes There, Lakes Everywhere

Lake County wasn't named after a person but for all of the large lakes within its territory.

NAMES AND PLACES

CITY NAMES

Yes! We Are Boring, but We're Not!
The small community called Boring is named for an early settler, W.H. Boring, and not for the social climate in the village. Residents claim that Boring is a very exciting place to live!

We're Not Inept, We're Talented!
Talent is named after Aaron Talent, who built the first general store in what became the downtown area. People would say that they were going to "Talent's" to get their mail and supplies, and eventually, the name stuck.

Horseradishes

Malin's name was inspired by a horseradish! In 1909, three representatives of an organization that sought suitable places for Czech immigrants to settle paid Oregon a visit, and soon, 50 members from Nebraska established a cooperative colony there. One of the settlers found a large, wild horseradish root growing nearby that reminded her of the famous horseradishes of Malin in Bohemia. Homesick perhaps, the group chose Malin as the name of their little community.

Italy

The city of Garibaldi is named after the Italian soldier and patriot Giuseppe Garibaldi, who unified Italy in the 1860s!

But if you thought that Florence was named after that big city in Italy, you'd be wrong! It's either in honor of state senator A.B. Florence or for a sunken lumber ship that bore the name.

You'd also be wrong if you thought Rome was named after the Italian capital. It's named after some nearby cliffs that early explorers called the "Walls of Rome."

NAMES AND PLACES

A Ditty About Death

William Hamilton named Elgin after the tune "Lost on the Lady Elgin," a once-popular ballad about a steamship that sank in Lake Michigan in 1860, killing more than 400 people.

Love Those Hotel Sheets!

Oregon's oldest ocean resort town, Seaside, was not named for its location, but for a luxury hotel. The Seaside House was built in the early 1870s, and for over 40 years, it catered to the rich and powerful of Portland and San Francisco. The Italian villa advertised itself as the oldest fashionable summer resort on the Oregon coast and included a racetrack and a stable of horses. Today, the hotel's grounds are the site of the Seaside Golf Club.

Spanish Towns

Manzanita takes its name from the fruit of the woollyleaf manzanita that grows locally. In Spanish, the word means "little apple."

Juntura is located near the place where the North Fork and Malheur Rivers combine. Its name is Spanish for "juncture."

Mulino is named after the flour mill built in the town in 1851. The Spanish word for mill is *Molino*, but the U.S. Postal Service wouldn't approve the correct spelling of the word for use as the town's name because it would be too easily confused with nearby Molalla.

Bonanza has nothing to do with the famous TV show. The city's name is Spanish for "prosperity."

Map Mistakes?

Christmas Valley takes its name from nearby Christmas Lake, but the lake is only nearby because of a mapmaker's mistake! Sometime between 1905 and 1912, the original Christmas Lake was renamed Hart Lake, and a new Christmas Lake—the one we know today—was christened.

DID YOU  KNOW?

Halfway was originally named because it was halfway between two mining towns. But in December 1999, the city accepted an offer from Half.com to add ".com" to its name for one year. The money from the deal went to the city, the local school and various non-profit groups.

Halfway's officials still get phone calls asking how it became the world's first dot.com city.

Ear Problem

Helix is probably the only city in the United States with a name inspired by a sore ear. The U.S. Postal Service rejected Oxford as the town's name because there were already too many of them in the country. A local resident suggested Helix instead. He'd heard the word while being treated for an ear infection. (The helix is part of the ear.)

Soda Anyone?
Sodaville got its name from a spring of pungent mineral water found on a nearby hillside in 1847. A city grew around the spring and, by the 1890s, both were popular tourist destinations that kept two hotels and several campsites filled during the summer. Today, Sodaville is largely a residential community.

Irregular Alignments

Zigzag is near Zigzag Canyon, Zigzag Mountain, Zigzag River and Zigzag Glacier. Where'd such a strange name come from? In 1845, explorer Joel Palmer left the following directions for a group of settlers who would have to navigate the ravine: "Turn directly to the right, go zigzag for about a hundred yards, then turn short round and go zigzag until you come under the place from which you started." The name stuck.

Biblical References

- Goshen is named after the pastoral region of Egypt where the ancient Israelites stayed before Moses led them into the Sinai.

- St. Paul is named after the Saint Paul Mission established there in 1839 by Francis Norbert Blanchet, the first Roman Catholic priest in Oregon and later the state's first archbishop.

- Ophir is named after a place that paid King Solomon gold, silver, ivory, precious stones, sandalwood, apes and peacocks as tribute.

Model Communities

There was a fierce debate in 1849 between two towns in Yamhill County over the location of a school that would serve both communities. Each wanted the building for their town. Eventually, the residents built a school somewhere in the middle. To honor this agreement, the school's first teacher called the school Amity, and the city that grew up around it took the name.

In the early 1890s, the ranchers peacefully settled on a new site for their post office despite fierce disagreements. They called the post office Unity, which became the name of the town that grew up around it.

The Civil War

Oregon's Union sympathies are reflected in a variety of place names:

- Grants Pass commemorates General Ulysses Grant's 1863 victory at Vicksburg.
- Sheridan was named after Civil War cavalry commander Philip Sheridan, who was stationed at forts near the city from 1856 to 1861.

Oregon's Confederate sympathizers named some places, too:

- Sumpter takes its name from a settlement founded in 1862 by five Confederate soldiers from South Carolina. The U.S. Post Office Department would not allow their original choice, Fort Sumter, which was the location of the Confederates' first victory in the Civil War.
- Tradition says that former Southerners living in Arlington, Oregon, in 1885 named their community to honor Robert E. Lee's home. Others claim the city was named for a local attorney.

NAMES AND PLACES

PLACES THAT REMIND PEOPLE OF HOME

Boston, Oregon?
Portland takes its name from Portland, Maine, the hometown of one of the city's founders. Many of Oregon's other communities are also named after residents' hometowns. Can you figure out where these Oregon place-names come from?

Albany	McMinnville
Ashland	Milwaukee
Bandon	Monmouth
Bay City	Moro
Dayton	Mt. Angel
Denmark	New Princeton
Detroit	Newberg
Dundee	Newport
Elmira	Ontario
Estacada	Paisley
Glasgow	Saginaw
Harrisburg	Scio
Independence	Sherwood
Lafayette	Toledo
Lebanon	Ukiah
Lexington	Wedderburn
Lostine	Weston
Lowell	

NAMES AND PLACES

Answers:

Albany . . . . Albany, New York
Ashland . . . . Ashland, Ohio
Bandon . . . . Bandon, Ireland
Bay City . . . . Bay City, Michigan
Dayton . . . . Dayton, Ohio
Denmark . . . . Kingdom of Denmark
Detroit . . . . Detroit, Michigan
Dundee . . . . Dundee, Scotland
Elmira . . . . Elmira, California
Estacada . . . . Llano Estacada, Texas
Glasgow . . . . Glasgow, Scotland
Harrisburg . . . . Harrisburg, Pennsylvania
Independence . . . . Independence, Missouri
Lafayette . . . . Lafayette, Indiana
Lebanon . . . . Lebanon, Tennessee
Lexington . . . . Lexington, Tennessee
Lostine . . . . Lostine, Kansas
Lowell . . . . Lowell, Maine
McMinnville . . . . McMinnville, Tennessee
Milwaukee . . . . Milwaukee, Wisconsin
Monmouth . . . . Monmouth, Illinois
Moro . . . . Moro, Illinois
Mount Angel . . . . Engelberg, Switzerland
New Princeton . . . . Princeton, Massachusetts
Newberg . . . . Neuberg, Germany
Newport . . . . Newport, Rhode Island
Norway . . . . Kingdom of Norway
Ontario . . . . Province of Ontario, Canada
Paisley . . . . Paisley, Scotland
Saginaw . . . . Saginaw, Michigan
Scio . . . . Scio, Ohio
Sherwood . . . . Sherwood, Michigan
Toledo . . . . Toledo, Ohio
Ukiah . . . . Ukiah, California
Wedderburn . . . . Wedderburn, Scotland
Weston . . . . Weston, Missouri

MYSTERIOUS NAMES

Sheep, Saints or Sagebrush
No one's sure how Nyssa got its name. It might be the acronym of the New York Sheep Shearing Association (or N.Y.S.S.A. for short). Or it might be the name a Union Pacific Railroad engineer's daughter. (She's said to have taken the name from St. Gregory of Nyssa.) Or, it might be the anglicized spelling of a Native American word for "sagebrush."

Sisters and Brothers
Sisters is named for the Three Sisters mountains 15 miles to the southwest. Brothers is more of a mystery. Was the community named for the higher than normal proportion of brothers that settled the area? Or was a rancher's name for his sheep camp, which became the name for the surrounding hills, adopted for the town's name? No one knows.

Not Where You Think
- Phoenix was named after the Phoenix Insurance Company of Hartford, Connecticut, not the Arizona town.

- Nashville is named after an early settler, not the home of the Grand Ole Opry.

- St. Louis was named after a log church that was built by settlers in 1845. Like St. Louis, Missouri, the parish was christened after the 13th-century French king, Louis IX.

- Mt. Vernon was not named for George Washington's Virginia plantation but in honor of a prized black stallion owned by an early settler.

- Madras was not named for the city in India, but for the cotton fabric that comes from the Chennai region around the city. The cloth was sold in a local store in 1903.

Island Paradise or Winter Wonderland?

Aloha is pronounced differently than the island greeting, but some say the name really does come from the Hawaiian word. Others insist the town is named after a Wisconsin resort on Lake Winnebago.

NAME CHANGES

Political Fight Over a Place of Peace

Salem takes its name from the Hebrew word for peace, *shalom*. The word was chosen early on to replace the Native American name for the area, *Chemeketa*, which is thought to mean "meeting place" or "resting place."

In 1853, residents submitted petitions to the territorial legislature calling for the name to be changed. Suggestions for replacements included Native American words such as "Chemeketa," "Woronoco" and "Multnomah." Others included "Thurston," "Corvallis" and "Bronson."

"Chemawa" was eventually approved by one branch of the legislature, and the matter was then sent to the territorial House of Representatives for a final vote. Instead, even more suggestions were made, and the vote never happened. Salem remained Salem.

Salem Almost Became Corvallis!
The name Corvallis was created by one of Marysville's earliest settlers by combining Latin words that together mean "heart of the valley." After efforts to rename Salem failed, Marysville took it on as its new name.

Brownsville, Take Two?

La Grande was originally named Brownsville until it was pointed out that there was already another town by that name in Linn County.

What's Wrong with Pigs?
Aumsville was once known as Hoggum because of the large number of pigs living in the area. It was later renamed by Henry Turner, a prominent early settler, for his dead son-in-law.

Don't Fire that Cannon!
For years, Cannon Beach residents couldn't agree on a name for their community. Some called it Elk Creek even though other Oregon towns used that name. Others called it Ecola. Finally, in 1922, the city was renamed Cannon Beach after a local beach named for the cannon that washed ashore after the sinking of the U.S. Navy survey schooner *Shark*.

Come On! Fess Up! Why Did You Do It?
In the 1880s, the Oregon & California Railroad planned to run its line across Bear Creek and to start a new town at the site. They named it Middle Ford, or Middleford, because of its location, but soon afterward O&CR railway engineer David Loring changed it to Medford. The fact that he was from Medford, Massachusetts, may have had something to do with it, but Loring claimed that he was just giving a new spelling to the old name: *mede* is an ancient word for medium, middle and middle land.

Tualatin Plain
What ever happened to the town of West Tualatin Plain? It was renamed Forest Grove. And how about East Tualatin Plain? That's now Hillsboro, but only after it was first called Columbia, Columbus and Hillsborough.

An Antelope, by Another Name...
The small city of Antelope was named after the animals that once grazed in the valley where the community is located. But in the early 1980s, followers of the Indian guru Bhagwan Shree Rajneesh started moving into Antelope and soon outnumbered the local residents. In 1984, by a vote of 57 to 22, with most of the Rajneeshees voting in favor of the proposal, the city changed its name to Rajneesh. In 1985, after the Bhagwan was deported and many of his leaders jailed, the town, including all of the remaining Rajneeshees, voted 34 to 0 to change the name back to Antelope.

HISTORIC HAPPENINGS

FIRSTS, OLDESTS, ETC.

Oldest in Oregon
The oldest community in Oregon is Celilo Village, but it's no longer the thriving community of salmon fishermen that it once. Only about 50 people live there year-round, twice that during fishing season.

DID YOU  KNOW?

Before Celilo Falls was inundated during the construction of The Dalles Dam in 1957, the hamlet was a major cultural and trading center. And archeologists have determined that Native Americans lived at Celilo at least as far back as 11,000 years ago. That makes it one of the longest continuously inhabited locations in North America.

Astoria: A City of Firsts
Astoria was founded in 1811, making it the first permanent non-Native settlement in the state. It started out as Fort Astoria, a fur trading post, and was incorporated in 1856.

The first United States Postal Service outlet west of the Rockies opened in Astoria in 1847, and the first United States customs house in Oregon was built there in 1849.

Another City of Firsts
Astoria may be older, but Oregon City can claim a number of impressive "firsts" as well:

- ☞ In 1844, Oregon City became the first city west of the Rocky Mountains to incorporate.
- ☞ It was the first capital of Oregon, serving as the seat of the provisional and territorial governments from 1844 to 1851.

- Oregon City had the state's first jail (1845), library (1845), newspaper (the *Oregon Spectator*, 1846) and mail delivery service (1846).
- Oregon City was also the first in the United States to have facilities for commercially transmitting electricity over long distances (1889) and the first to have a public elevator (1915).

DID YOU KNOW?

Oregon City was the first city in the United States to have multi-life navigational locks. Built in 1873, the Willamette Locks lift barges and ships 40 feet from the lower half of Willamette River to its upper half, allowing the vessels to go around Willamette Falls and travel up and down the river. The locks are also the oldest navigational locks in the United States that are still in use.

You Can Mine Our Gold, But You Can't Own Our Land
Jacksonville was the site of Oregon's first Chinatown. The Chinese miners moved north from San Francisco when gold was discovered in southern Oregon in 1851. They paid a tax in order to mine the gold there, but they were not allowed to own any land.

What Are They Teaching in Condon?
Two of Oregon's three Nobel laureates—William P. Murphy and Linus Pauling—were raised in Condon. The third, Carl Wieman, is from Corvallis.

Don't Fence Me In!
Butte Falls is the only city in the United States to have a fence that goes around the entire city. It's also the only one where you have to go through a cattle guard to get into town. People say the fence is there to keep all the free-range cattle and cows that surround Butte Falls from just walking into town.

Gallium
McDermitt is the site of the largest gallium deposits in North America. Gallium is a soft and brittle, silver-colored metal that melts when held in the palm of your hand. Ninety-five percent of all gallium is used in electronics. Gallium is now produced as a by-product of aluminum and zinc processing, but Gold Canyon Resources is thinking of developing the site, and if enough investors sign on, McDermitt will become the site of the world's only gallium mine.

Let Us Hear You Sing!
The world's tallest barbershop pole is in Forest Grove! At 72 feet tall, it is located in Lincoln Park just north of the Pacific University campus. The pole was donated to the city by barbershop singers from Portland in honor of Forest Grove's role in preserving and encouraging the art of barbershop quartet singing. The town is known as "Ballad Town USA," and every year since 1947, the Gleemen of Forest Grove has sponsored a barbershop quartet competition that draws contestants from across the country.

No Bride
Bridal Veil was the site of the state's first paper mill, which was built in 1886. The community is now a ghost town.

Small City Park
Salem is home to one of the world's smallest city parks. In 1872, William Waldo, a prominent attorney and judge, planted a redwood tree on his property near where Summer and Union Streets now meet. Years later, he sold the land with the stipulation that the tree be preserved. In 1936, the city designated the 12-foot by 20-foot plot surrounding the tree Waldo Park. Today, the tree stands 82 feet tall and has a trunk that's six feet in diameter.

OREGON'S AWESOME! A 90-foot-high bluff divides Oregon City's central business district near the beach from the residential neighborhood above. In the early 1950s, an elevator was built to connect the two. It replaced an elevator that had been constructed 40 years earlier as well as a stairway that was built in the 1860s and a trail that was first used by Native Americans years before that. The current structure is the only outdoor municipal elevator in the United States and is one of only four outdoor elevators in the world. At the top of the elevator is a flying saucer-shaped observation deck overlooking Willamette Falls. The elevator is also one of the few left that is still manually run by a human operator. There is no charge for its use.

Oregon's First Planned City

Hines was Oregon's first preplanned community. In 1929, construction started in nearby Burns on a large mill owned by the Edward Hines Lumber Company. The mill would employ more people than Burns could house, so the company hired three realtors from Mississippi to buy 2000 acres around the mill and to plan and develop a subdivision with houses, schools, a park and other amenities. The city of Burns was supposed to annex the development but couldn't raise the $1 million needed to reimburse the realtors for what they had invested. So the realtors met in 1930 and formed their own city.

One-Way Streets

Eugene was the first city in the United States to have one-way streets. Its system of alternating one-way streets in the downtown core began in 1945 and was designed by Eugene's first city manager, Deane Seeger.

DID YOU  KNOW?

The Oregon State Highway Division once did a study of one-way streets and what they discovered may surprise you. While one-way streets have, on average, 23 percent more traffic than their two-way counterparts, they also have 10 percent fewer accidents!

Oregon's Smallest City

Greenhorn was established during the eastern Oregon gold rush of the 1860s and had about 3200 residents by 1895. Incorporated in 1903, the community survived until World War II, when the War Production Board in 1942 put an end to all nonessential mining in the country, including gold mining. Most of the townsfolk left shortly thereafter, and for decades, the city had no permanent residents! There were some winter cabins and summer vacation homes, and a few part-time residents lived out of their RVs, but no one stayed year-round.

That all changed in 2003 when a couple from Eugene, Joyce Papel and Ron Bergstrom, built a new home and made the city their full-time residence. Their water is pumped in from a mountain spring, they generate their own electricity, and telephone service comes via an underground cable. They use snowmobiles in the winter to get to Baker City and John Day for supplies.

Other Greenhorn Facts

- Greenhorn is also Oregon's smallest city in terms of area. Its city limits encompass only 54.4 acres!

- The mayor is Frances Villwock, and she lives 200 miles away in Mill City.

- Greenhorn's jailhouse has been on exhibit at the Grant County Historical Museum in Canyon City since 1963.

- At 6410 feet above sea level, Greenwood has the highest elevation of any incorporated city in Oregon!

OREGON'S AWESOME! In November 2006, 18-year-old Kyle Corbin was elected to a two-year term as mayor of Union after a write-in campaign that garnered him 415 votes. He ran a write-in campaign because the city charter requires candidates to be "qualified electors" by the September filing deadline, but he was only 17 at the time. The young politician turned 18 five weeks before the election, making him the second youngest mayor currently serving in the United States and probably the youngest in Oregon history.

The former Union High School student body president is currently a student at Eastern Oregon University where he studies political science, philosophy and economics, but you can find him at his office in Union's City Hall every Wednesday from 1:00 to 3:30 PM and from 6:00 to 7:30 PM.

Are You Sure You're the Tallest?

At 4798 feet, Lakeview claims to be the "Tallest Town in Oregon." Greenhorn's taller but, with about 3000 residents, Lakeview is certainly the "tallest" town of any real size.

Wanna Catch Bigfoot?

The only government-sanctioned Bigfoot trap is located in the Rogue River National Forest. It was built in 1974 after a short-lived group called North American Wildlife Research got a special use permit from the federal government to construct a 10 by 10-square-foot trap. So far, Bigfoot hasn't been caught, but be careful if you go looking for the trap! It's made of creosoted planks and posts with reinforced steel bolts and is anchored to large lumber pillars. Even today, if you spring the trap, it won't be easy to get out!

HISTORIC HAPPENINGS

GHOST TOWNS

Heaps of History
Oregon has hundreds of ghost towns. Some even say that it has more than any other state! There is at least one ghost town in Oregon for every city, town and community that still survives. For most of these once thriving but now gone communities, nothing is left but memories, photographs and perhaps a road, a marker or a piece of old machinery.

Ghost Town Along the Willamette
Champoeg is arguably the most important ghost town in Oregon's history. Halfway between Oregon City and Salem, it was an important meeting place, first for Native Americans and, later, for the Hudson's Bay Company's French-Canadian voyageurs. Beginning in 1829, retired fur trappers and their families built the Willamette Valley's first farms there. By the late 1850s, the fledgling town had grown to approximately 50 buildings—among them was the valley's first gristmill—and boasted 200 residents. An important crossroads, in 1843, settlers met there and voted to form a provisional government, the first step towards becoming a part of the United States.

Champoeg's glory ended on December 2, 1861, when the Willamette had its worst flood in recorded history. The river rose 55 feet above its summer flood stage, covering the town in seven feet of water. Part of the town was rebuilt, but another flood in 1890 finished the job, destroying the town for good. Today, nothing is left of the original town, but a state park is maintained on the site.

Valsetz (b. 1919, d. 1984)

A timber company established this community in 1919 as a place for its employees to live, and up to 1500 people eventually lived there. There were churches, stores, a post office and a newspaper. The high school football team even made it to the state playoffs. But the local old-growth timber was eventually depleted and, in 1983, Boise Cascade, who owned the entire town, closed it down.

Townsfolk were told to find work elsewhere and were moved out. Their homes, as well as the other buildings in Valsetz, were all bulldozed. What remained was burned, and the land was planted over with Douglas fir trees. Today, only one structure survives, and the site is part of the Valsetz Tree Farm. Every year, former residents meet at Falls City for a reunion.

Glad They Didn't Make It the State Capitol!

Seven miles south of Baker City was the community of Auburn. Established in 1862 after gold was found at nearby Griffin Gulch, it went from two log buildings to a population of between 5000 and 6000 in only a matter of months, making it the second largest city in the state! Auburn became the first county seat when Baker County was established that September, and some people talked seriously about moving the state capitol there. In 1864, however, the gold began to run out, and so did the people. Only 150 residents were left by the end of that year, and the town was largely deserted by the 1870s. The last of its buildings disappeared sometime before 1945.

HISTORIC HAPPENINGS

Vanport Floods

At one time, the fastest growing city in Oregon in the 20th century was Vanport. Located between Portland and the Columbia River, the community was built virtually overnight in 1943 and consisted almost entirely of hastily constructed public housing for the people coming to Oregon to work at the shipyards in Portland and Vancouver, Washington, during World War II. At one time, Vanport had 50,000 residents, making it the second largest city in the state!

But in late May 1948, record rains caused the river to rise 23 feet above flood stage, putting parts of Vanport were under 15 feet of water! Then shortly after 4:00 PM on May 30, a 200-foot section of the dike protecting residents from the river collapsed, sending a 10-foot-high wall of water into the city. In only a few hours, the entire community was flooded. All of its 18,500 residents were immediately homeless, and 16 people were killed. Vanport was a total loss, and no attempt was made to rebuild. Today, Delta Park, the Portland International Raceway, the Heron Lakes Golf Course and rail station are located on the site.

Ghost Town that's Underwater
Not all of Oregon's ghost towns are above ground. The coastal community of Bayocean near Cape Meares was swallowed up bit by bit by the sea when ocean currents shifted.

What's In a Name?

The names of Oregon's ghost towns were as varied and interesting as those of the cities, towns, and communities that now survive. Some especially interesting ones are Glad Tidings, New Era, Jawbone Flats and Idiotville.

HISTORIC HAPPENINGS

Not Yet a Ghost Town

Bridal Veil, located in Multnomah County in the Columbia Gorge, was established in 1886 as a logging company town. After all the nearby trees were cut down, the community's main industry became the making of wooden cheese boxes for Kraft Foods. But Kraft left Bridal Veil in 1960, and the last mill closed in 1988. In 2001, the mill houses and most of the other buildings in Bridal Veil were torn down. All that remains is a post office, a church and a cemetery. But Bridal Veil refuses to become a ghost town. Each year, thousands of brides visit the town to drop off their wedding invitations at the post office to have them stamped with the Bridal Veil postmark. Some of them surely stop to have their photo taken in front of the church.

World War II Cities

Camp Adair was the largest military training camp in Oregon during orld War II. Located north of Corvallis, the camp had training grounds, artillery ranges and a simulated Japanese village. There were also 1800 buildings, including barracks, mess halls, offices, five movie theaters, seven churches and a bakery that produced 35,000 loaves of bread every day! Camp Adair also contained a military hospital that cared for 3600 patients. From August 1944 to April 1946, it served as a prisoner of war camp for captured German and Italian soldiers.

Over 100,000 soldiers went through Camp Adair's gates and, at its height, it had a population of at least 35,000, making it, for a short time, Oregon's second largest city. No longer needed after the war, Camp Adair was declared surplus property in December 1945 and demolition began two years later. It took a decade to tear down or move the buildings. The site is now home to the city of Adair Village.

Camp Adair wasn't the only military city in Oregon during the war. Camp White was a training center near Medford that encompassed 77 square miles and was, at one time, home to nearly 40,000 men.

Camp Abbott, 11 miles south of Bend, was an Engineer Replacement Training Center. Even though it was open only 14 months, up to 10,000 men at a time—90,000 in all—passed through its gates.

City of Wealth and Plenty

Perhaps the ghost town with the most optimistic name was Cornucopia. The word means "wealth" and "plenty," and that certainly describes the old town east of Baker City. The precious gold ore was mined there until World War II, and there are stories from the 1880s and 1890s of gold being so plentiful that it literally fell out of the rock wherever a miner's pick fell. Millions of dollars of gold ore were taken out of the ground at Cornucopia. There are no permanent residents there now, but much of the town remains, and there are a number of summer homes, too.

But for the Alps

Whitney's population was never more than 100. But near the lumber town was the second highest trestle in the world! Only the Bavarian Alps has one that's higher. Whitney was located about a half-mile south of Highway 7 near Austin, but was abandoned after a fire destroyed much of it in 1918. The three-story sawmill remains as do a number of empty homes, but they're all on private property, so please don't trespass.

HISTORIC HAPPENINGS

FOUNDING MOTHERS AND FATHERS

Mother of Oregon

Tabitha Moffatt Brown, also known as the "Mother of Oregon," received this honor from the state legislature in 1987. She was a feisty woman who, in 1846, at the age of 66, made the trek from Missouri to Oregon under her own steam—and on her own coin. Her mission was to travel west and establish a home for orphaned children of pioneer immigrants. Grandma Brown, as she quickly came to be known, was said to represent "the distinctive pioneer heritage and the charitable and compassionate nature of Oregon's people."

HISTORIC HAPPENINGS

Father of Oregon

Dr. John McLoughlin, also known as the "Father of Oregon," received the honor from the state legislature in 1957. Born in 1784 in Rivière-du-Loup, Québec, and schooled in both Canada and Scotland, he earned a degree and license to practice surgery and pharmacy before he was 19 years old! He accepted a position as medical officer for the North West Fur Company and moved to Oregon, where he became a trader and learned the language of several Native American tribes.

In 1814, he became a partner in the company he served and played a key role in its merger with the Hudson's Bay Company. By 1824, he was in charge of the area that would became known as the Oregon Territory. As chief factor for the region, he took charge of the Bay Company's Fort George in Astoria and built Fort Vancouver near present-day Vancouver, Washington. He also helped the American settlers who arrived in Oregon in the 1840s and turned Fort Vancouver into a thriving commercial center. McLoughlin died in 1857.

DID YOU  KNOW?

Dr. McLoughlin refused to leave Oregon when the territory was divided between Great Britain and the United States in 1846. Instead, he moved to Oregon City and became an American citizen in 1849. Two years later, he became the city's mayor for two years. His house in Oregon City is now a national historic site, and his grave is just beside the building, which is said to be haunted!

Mountain Man

Sam Barlow and his family moved west to Oregon in 1845, but instead of making the last leg of the journey via the Columbia River, he decided to continue over the Cascade Mountains. His determination, and his belief that God must have made a way over that mountain, paid off and today, Barlow Pass is named in his honor.

One year later, he retraced his journey and convinced the government to build a toll road. It opened in 1846. Travelers looking to pass with a team of horses were charged $5, along with an added fee of $1 per head—cattle or person! Unfortunately, most pioneers couldn't afford the toll fee and were either allowed to pass by a kindhearted attendant or turned away. In the end, the toll idea was ditched, and the State of Oregon took over ownership of the road in 1919.

While the road may not have produced the financial revenue its founder had hoped for, about 75 percent of the early Willamette Valley settlers were believed to have passed this way.

HISTORIC HAPPENINGS

TRAVELING THE OREGON TRAIL

A Legacy

As a young man, Ezra Meeker headed out west and successfully made his way to Oregon in 1852. Then in 1906, at the age of 76, he decided to retrace his steps to encourage the preservation of the Oregon Trail. It was no easy feat—of the two oxen he'd chosen to help him on his trip, only one made it to their destination alive! But it seemed worth it when President Teddy Roosevelt promised money for the project.

Having received such a positive response, Meek continued to travel back and forth on the trail to raise awareness for his cause until his death at the ripe old age of 98!

DID YOU KNOW?

Narcissa Whitman and Eliza Spaulding were the first white women to travel across the Rockies on their way to Oregon.

Pioneer Visionary

Jesse Applegate and his family were members of the first wave of the Great Migration of 1843. They were among the 120 wagons, 875 people and more than 1000 head of livestock setting out from Independence, Missouri.

In 1844, after settling in Oregon City, Applegate got busy building a mill and surveying the townsite. A year later, he served in the provisional government and later backed Abraham Lincoln in his bid for the presidency. But most importantly, Applegate played a significant role in opening a southern route by which other immigrants could come to Oregon. That path is named the Applegate Trail in his honor.

HISTORIC HAPPENINGS

A Voice for Women

Abigail Jane Scott (Duniway) was just 17 when she accompanied her family from Illinois over the Oregon Trail in 1852. Both her mother and youngest brother died on the journey. A keen and successful student, Abigail taught at the school in Eola.

She married at 19, but when her husband was crippled in an accident a decade later, she was forced to provide for her family. Through this experience, she became aware of the legal inequalities endured by women. In 1871, the family moved to Portland, and for 17 years, Abigail advocated for equal rights in a weekly newspaper called the *New Northwest*. She was Oregon's first woman newspaper publisher, and her efforts helped women get the vote in Oregon, Idaho and Washington.

Gold Fever Facts

- It is estimated that two-thirds of the men in Oregon left for California when the gold rush began there in 1848.

- One of these gold-seeking Oregonians, Peter Burnett, became governor of California in 1849.

- Southwest Oregon had a gold rush of its own soon after 1848. Another followed in the northeast in the 1860s.

- Since the first days of the Gold Rush in 1848, at least six million ounces of gold has been dug up in Oregon.

- The largest gold nugget weighed in at 17 pounds and was discovered in 1859 at Althouse Creek in Josephine County. A few years later a pretty impressive runner-up was uncovered. It weighed 15 pounds.

- Two-thirds of the gold found in Oregon has come from Baker County.

DID YOU  KNOW?

The California Gold Rush was actually a boon to Oregon's economy because it created a market for Oregon's products other than furs. It also brought gold to the state! Before the rush of 1848, the most common currency among Oregon settlers was wheat. One bushel was worth one dollar. Try carrying that in your wallet!

The Coastal Route

The most bizarre route from New York to Oregon was an ocean voyage that took travelers to their destination via the Antarctic! Yup, that meant rounding the tip of South America and then heading back north to Oregon.

Apparently, settlers wanting to avoid a four-month overland journey on foot regularly opted for the yearlong ocean trip despite the fact that the costs were astronomical and many ships were so unseaworthy that they sank before reaching their destination!

Footwear

The Oregon Trail runs roughly 2170 miles. But whether they were youngsters, pregnant women or elderly gents, early settlers had to walk most of the way there, which meant they chewed up a whole lot of shoes. In 1853, one settler, May Ellen Murdock Compton, wrote in her diary that she'd gone through nine of the 10 pairs of new shoes she'd packed for the trip and only managed saving that 10th pair by walking the final leg of her journey barefoot!

The Price of Adventure

For early settlers, everything was more expensive out west. According to one source, the cost of flour skyrocketed from $4 a barrel in the Midwest to an alarming $1 per pint in Oregon. Sugar and coffee cost $1.50 and $1 per pint, respectively!

Tidbits from the Oregon Trail

- It cost pioneers heading west between $800 and $1000 to purchase supplies and equip their wagons.
- The leading cause of death among pioneers traversing the Oregon Trail was cholera.
- One in five women making their way along the trail was pregnant, and almost all traveled with small children.
- Of the men traveling west, 60 percent were farmers, 20 percent were craftsmen or merchants and 12 percent were doctors, lawyers, teachers or other professionals.
- One-fifth of Oregon's settlers came from Missouri.

ECONOMY

THE BASICS

Oregon's Economic Engine
With its rich natural resources, thousands of acres of farmland and strong manufacturing sectors, Oregon's economy provides jobs for millions of people and makes products that are shipped around the world. In 2005, it produced a total of $144.3 billion in goods and services.

ECONOMY

DID YOU  KNOW?

In 2006, the largest group of Oregon's workers were employed in the food services industry. Other important employers are hospitals, contractors and the computer and electronics industry.

The Best Places to Work in Oregon

Oregon Business magazine has compiled a list of the top 100 best companies to work for in Oregon.

The top 10 large companies:

    U.S. Cellular Wireless
    Microsoft Corporation
    Qualcomm Wireless
    Carr Auto Group
    Edge Wireless
    Evanta
    Walsh Construction
    Pacific Continental Bank
    MulvannyG2 Architecture
    Point B Solutions Group

The top 10 small companies:

    River City Travel
    Columbia Printing and Graphics
    United Risk Solutions
    Bridge City Legal
    Performance Health Technology
    Staff Finders Technical of Oregon
    Pittman & Brooks
    Grady Britton
    Reitmeier Mechanical
    Quango Design & Marketing

ECONOMY

The Best Places to Work in Oregon
In 2007, three Oregon companies made it onto *Fortune Magazine*'s list of the 100 best companies to work for in the United States—Umpqua Bank, Perkins Coie (a law firm) and Nike.

DID YOU  KNOW?

Inc. magazine has ranked the Medford region as the fifth best place in the country to do business.

Small Business

In 2006, 50 percent of Oregon's private sector workforce was employed at businesses that had fewer than 100 employees. That includes the 25 percent who worked at firms employing less than 20 people.

The numbers are even more impressive when seen from the point of view of the more than 100,000 businesses in Oregon—98 percent of them employ fewer than 100 people.

International Trade

- In 2005, Oregon exported $12.3 billion in products to other counties.

- One in four manufacturing jobs in Oregon are linked to international trade.

- The top exports were computers and electronics, transportation equipment and agricultural products.

- The state's top 10 foreign markets in 2005 included Canada, South Korea and Japan.

ECONOMY

AGRICULTURE, FORESTRY AND FISHING

Quick Facts
According to 2002 figures from the United States Department of Agriculture:

- There are 40,033 farms in Oregon, and a total of 17,080,422 acres of land is used for agriculture. The average size of a farm is 427 acres.
- The top agricultural exports are vegetables, wheat and fruit.
- Oregon farmers produce almost $10 million of organic goods.

Oregon's Favorite Fruit

Oregon named the pear its state fruit in 2005. Here are some interesting facts about this tasty treat:

- Pears are the number one tree fruit grown in Oregon.

- Oregon grows about 800 million pears per year. That's enough to supply every person in the state with about 294 pears!

- Oregon's pears are exported to more than 40 countries.

Cranberry Central

Thirty million pounds of cranberries are grown every year near Bandon. That's 95 percent of the state's cranberries and five percent of the national crop.

DID YOU  KNOW?

Oregon is the fourth largest producer of cranberries in the United States. And we've been growing the stuff ever since Charles McFarlin brought cranberry vines here from Massachusetts in 1885. There's even a cranberry variety named McFarlin in his honor.

Logging and Lumber

Oregon produces more than five billion board feet of lumber per year. Logging and wood processing have long been major industries in Oregon, but in an effort to protect wildlife living in its many forests—and especially in old-growth areas—many woodlands have been closed to logging.

Not a Fish Story

In 2006, Oregon's commercial fishers caught nearly 17,000 tons of Dungeness crab and 900 tons of salmon. All told the salmon was worth nearly $5 million. The crab was valued at almost $54 million!

ECONOMY

BY THE NUMBERS

Median Income
According to the U.S. Census Bureau in 2003, the median income for a family of four in Oregon was $61,570.

Oregon ranked 30th when compared with other states. New Jersey came in at the top spot with $87,412, and New Mexico ranked lowest with $45,867. The national median income for a family of four was $65,093.

Of course, not everyone lives in a family of four. The overall median household income (regardless of family size) in Oregon in 2003 was $42,593. That compares to the national median household income of $43,318. The nation's high was Connecticut with $56,409, and the low was Mississippi at $32,397.

County by County

In 2000, only nine of Oregon's 36 counties had a median household wage greater than the state's average. The top five counties in 2000 were:

Washington	$52,122
Clackamas	$52,080
Columbia	$45,797
Yamhill	$44,111
Polk	$42,311

The bottom five counties in 2000 were:

Lake	$29,506
Curry	$30,117
Malheur	$30,241
Baker	$30,367
Harney	$30,957

Income Distribution

Only New York has a bigger gap between its rich and poor than Oregon. Here are a few stats on the matter:

☛ At last count, the top 20 percent of Oregon families enjoyed 10 times the income of the poorest 20 percent.

☛ Between the late 1970s and the late 1990s, the poorest fifth of families saw their annual average income decrease by $430 to $14,150. It has since gone down even further.

☛ During the same period, the richest fifth of Oregonian families saw their incomes increase by $48,260 to $141,430.

Poverty Report
Of Oregon's total population, 12 percent lived below the poverty line in 2003. That's lower than the national average of 12.5 percent but slightly higher than Idaho and Washington rates.

What is Poverty?
The U.S. Department of Health and Human Services set the poverty line for a family of four in 2006 at $20,000. For an individual, it's $9800.

Oregon's Poor
In Oregon, Malheur County has the highest rate of poverty at 18.3 percent. Clackamas County has the least at 8.4 percent.

Who is most likely to live in poverty? Families headed by single mothers with children under the age of five. According to the American Community Survey, 56.5 percent of them live below the poverty threshold. African Americans, Native Americans and Hispanics are also among the hardest hit.

Homeless
In 2005, 10,528 Oregonians asked to stay the night in a homeless shelter.

A Roof Over Your Head
In 2004, about 64 percent of Oregonians owned their own homes, slightly under the national average of 66.2 percent. The median cost of a home was $152,100.

Oregonians Move a Lot
Only 46.8 percent of Oregonians reported during the 2000 census that they were living in the same house they resided in just five years before. Where had they been living before?

Overseas	2.6 percent
Different State	12.5 percent
Different County	23.6 percent
Same County, Different House	27.0 percent

Minimum Wage Rates
Oregon's minimum wage is $7.80 an hour, a full $2.65 above the federal minimum. Only Washington's is higher. Since 2004, the minimum wage in Oregon has been tied to inflation and automatically goes up every January with the amount rounded off to the nearest nickel. Here are a few state comparisons:

State	Minimum wage
Washington	$7.93
Oregon	$7.80
California	$7.50
Nevada	$6.15
Federal minimum wage	$5.15

Twenty-four states follow the federal guideline.

DID YOU  KNOW?

Only six states have minimum wages that are below that of the federal government. In Kansas, the minimum wage is a mere $2.65 an hour. And there is no minimum wage at all in Alabama, Louisiana, Mississippi, South Carolina and Tennessee! Fortunately, most employees in those states are covered by the federal statute.

Who Earns the Lower Wages?
More than half of the employees in Oregon who earn less than $8 an hour work in the leisure and hospitality trade or in retail.

Unemployment Rates—A History

Oregon's unemployment rate was fairly constant during most of the 1990s, but from 2000 to 2003, it jumped by nearly 59 percent! For those three years, Oregon had the highest annual average unemployment rate of any state in the country. Only in 2006 did it go back down.

Highs and Lows
In 2006, the annual average unemployment rate was under five percent in only three counties:

Washington	4.5 percent
Benton	4.7 percent
Clackamas	4.8 percent

It was over eight percent in two counties:

Grant	8.4 percent
Harney	8.2 percent

ECONOMY

DID YOU KNOW?

Oregon is one of the most expensive states to live in, with an overall cost of living that is about 10 percent higher than the national average. But Oregonians pay fewer taxes per capita than most other Americans. The average Oregonian spent more money for hunting and fishing licenses ($11.21 per capita) than on property taxes ($6.71).

Tax Free!

Oregon has no sales tax! Only four other states can make that claim—Alaska, Delaware, Montana and New Hampshire.

ECONOMY

OREGON'S BUSINESSES MEAN BUSINESS!

Old-Time Industrial Site in Mulino!
The oldest industrial building in Oregon is the wooden frame Howard's Grist Mill in Mulino. It was built in 1851 and was used for over 100 years to mill grain and flour as well as poultry and dairy feeds. It also served as the town's post office.

Oldest Businesses

☛ When it was sold in 2002, Hauke's Sentry Market in Astoria was the oldest continuously family-owned grocery store west of the Rocky Mountains. It was established in 1890.

☛ Gimre's Shoes in Astoria is the oldest continuously family-owned shoe store west of the Mississippi. It opened in 1892 and is still in business today.

☛ The Butteville General Store near Aurora is the oldest operating general store in Oregon. It first opened in 1863 and, except for two years in the late 1990s, has operated ever since.

☛ Established in 1852, Henry Saxer's Liberty Brewery in Portland is Oregon's largest and oldest brewing company. In 1862, Saxer sold the brewery to Henry Weinhard, who founded one of Oregon's biggest beer companies.

DID YOU  KNOW?

The Wolf Creek Inn is the oldest continuously operating hotel in the Pacific Northwest. Built in 1883, Jack London finished his novel *Valley of the Moon* there, and the mountain behind the inn is called London Peak in his honor. Other visitors have included Clark Gable, Mary Pickford, Douglas Fairbanks, Carol Lombard and Orson Wells.

ECONOMY

OREGON'S AWESOME! After lobbying the Oregon legislature to make brewpubs legal, brothers Mike and Brian McMenamin opened the McMenamin's Hillsdale Brewery and Public House in Portland in 1984. It has since grown into the third largest brewpub chain in the United States, with 54 breweries and brewpubs across Oregon and Washington. They serve more than 20,000 barrels of beer each year! The McMenamin brothers are famous for placing their brewpubs in historic but abandoned buildings that they have renovated using bizarre artifacts and wonderful pieces of art. Nine of their locations are on the National Register of Historic Places!

Sportswear

The world's largest supplier of athletic shoes, clothing and equipment is Beaverton's Nike, Inc. The company was founded in 1964 by the former University of Oregon track and field star Phil Knight and his coach, the famous Bill Bowerman. They each chipped in $500 and began with Knight selling shoes from the back of his station wagon. Today, the business earns $15 billion a year, employs more than 23,000 workers and has three subsidiaries.

DID YOU  KNOW?

Portland State University graphic design student Carolyn Davidson designed Nike's famous Swoosh logo in 1971. Nike founder and part-time PSU accounting instructor Phil Knight hired her for a few dollars an hour to do some charts, graphs and other work for his fledgling company. One day, he told Davidson that he needed a logo. Davidson came up with the Swoosh and was paid $35 for it. In 1983, she made good with a gold, Swoosh-shaped diamond ring and an undisclosed amount of Nike stock.

The Truth is Out!
The 2001 movie, *A Knight's Tale*, invents a different story to explain the creation of Nike's Swoosh. In the movie, a 14th-century blacksmith puts the mark on her suits of armor so that other knights will recognize the gear as her handiwork.

DID YOU  KNOW?

Nike takes its name from the Greek goddess of victory.

Oregonian Innovation
An innovative company called Pacific Yurts Inc. has modernized 19th-century Mongolian and Turkish tents and now sells them to individuals and to the Oregon Department of Parks and Recreation. There are now 159 yurts for rent in 19 different Oregon parks.

Antiques and Used Books

There are so many antique shops and used bookstores in Lincoln City that *Country Home Magazine* has named the city one of the 10 best-kept "antique" secrets in the United States.

Let's Shop in Woodburn!
The Woodburn Company Stores is the largest outlet mall in the Pacific Northwest. Opening in 1999, the 300,000 square foot mall attracts over four million shoppers every year

Can't Do Business Without Ladd's Banks

Portland businessman William S. Ladd and San Francisco entrepreneur Charles E. Tilton established the Ladd and Tilton Bank in Portland in 1859. It was the first bank north of Sacramento and west of Salt Lake City. The Ladd and Tilton no longer exists; it disappeared when it was purchased by the United States National Bank (now known as US Bank) in 1925.

Architectural Buffs—Go Visit a Bank!
From 1868 to 1911, the Ladd and Tilton Bank in Portland was located in a magnificent building with a cast-iron façade based on the Liberia Vecchia of Venice, Italy. It was torn down in 1954, and the site is now a 100-car parking lot. But don't despair! US Bank's Ladd and Bush branch in Salem has cast-iron facades cast from the same molds as those of its Portland cousin.

DID YOU  KNOW?

In 1970, the United States National Bank was the first bank in Oregon to install automated teller machines.

The Largest Bank in Oregon?

The US Bank, which was originally headquartered in Portland, has almost 2500 branches in 24 states and is the largest bank in Oregon and the sixth largest in the United States. It now operates out of Minneapolis.

Oregon's largest community-based bank is the Umpqua Bank. Founded in Canyonville in 1953, it now has 64 branches across the state and $2.6 billion in assets.

What's Is It about Banks and Tall Buildings?
The 546-foot-high Wells Fargo Center in Portland is the tallest building in the state. The second tallest is another bank building: the 526-foot-tall US Bancorp Tower in Portland.

Can't Do Business Without Lawyers!

George B. Currey was admitted to the Oregon bar in 1858, settled in McMinnville and tried his first case two years later. In 1868, he took on a young attorney by the name of Harwell

Hurley as a partner. The business remains in operation, despite some name changes, and is Oregon's oldest law firm.

The largest law firm in the state is Stoel Rives. There are over 160 lawyers in its Portland office and another 200 attorneys work in eight offices across California, Nevada, Idaho and Washington. Stoel Rives was also recently voted "Oregon's Most Admired Company" in a *Portland Business Journal* poll of 800 of the state's top CEOs.

Milk and Ice Cream
Three times in the last 10 years, Roseburg's Umpqua Dairy has won the prestigious Irving B. Weber Award, the highest honor that a Quality Chekd dairy can receive.

That's a Lot of Tires!

The second largest chain of tire stores in the United States is Oregon's Les Schwab Tires. It all started when a 34-year old native of Bend (named Les Schwab, of course!) bought a small OK Rubber Welders tire store in Prineville in 1952. Today, it's an empire that includes over 400 stores and 7000 employees across seven states and does more than $1.5 billion in business every year. The company is also known for its strict dress code, the fact that all of its outlets are closed on Sundays and its "Free Beef" promotion every February.

CULINARY ADVENTURES

TEMPTING THE TASTE BUDS

Spaghetti Surprise

People told Guss Dussin that a spaghetti restaurant would never work. He ignored them and opened the first Old Spaghetti Factory restaurant in Portland in 1969. Today, with 37 outlets in 14 states, over 10 million customers are served every year, making the Old Spaghetti Factory the most successful pasta-based restaurant chain in the United States!

DID YOU  KNOW?

Guss Dussin's wife, Sally, decorated their first restaurant with whatever she could buy cheap from garage sales and other sources. She still supervises the decorating of every Old Spaghetti Factory restaurant, spending up to $1 million on antiques, reproductions and other interior improvements. There's an old-fashioned streetcar at every location.

A Hamburger with a Cause

Twenty-four of Burgerville USA's 39 restaurants are in Oregon, so you might be surprised to learn the chain opened in Vancouver, Washington! Still, there's a big Oregon connection. Most of the beef comes from Oregon's cattle, and the cheese is from Tillamook. The menu also includes Oregon hazelnut and Rogue River blue cheese salads and milkshakes with Oregon-made ice cream and marionberries.

But Burgerville is also a company with a social conscience. It uses only antibiotic and hormone-free beef, free-range turkey and eggs from uncaged hens. It avoids all trans fats, 100 percent of its power comes from local windmills, and it turns its used cooking oil into biodiesel fuel!

DID YOU  KNOW?

Gourmet magazine selected Burgerville as "America's Freshest Fast Food" in 2003.

Ice Cream Heaven
The K & R Drive-In at Rice Hill is easily the most famous roadside diner in Oregon. They've got hamburgers and fries, but they're known for their 37 flavors of delicious Oregon-made Umpqua ice cream. And they're generous with it! A small cone has two giant scoops, the large has six! One food critic called K & R an "Ice Cream Nirvana."

Pizza Research Institute
With its delicious combinations of toppings that constantly change and that you will never find anywhere else, the vegetarian and vegan friendly Pizza Research Institute has a near-cult following in Eugene. Examples? A pizza with thin slices of crisp Fuji apples topped with smoked gouda or another with peaches, apricots and corn! Mmmm, good.

Mexi-Oregon
Ron Fraedrick opened the first TacoTime next door to the University of Oregon campus in Eugene in 1960 after mortgaging his house and borrowing another $5000 to get started. Fraedrick fell in love with Mexican cuisine while in Southern California and was determined to bring tacos and other delights from south of the border to the hungry college students at his alma mater. That first TacoTime was a two-window walk-up restaurant. Today, there are more than 300 locations in the United States, Canada and Japan.

CULINARY ADVENTURES

DID YOU  KNOW?

Ron Fraedrick used to mix his secret combination of seasonings and spices in a 55-gallon barrel every night after closing. To make sure everything blended properly, he'd roll the barrel around the parking lot a couple of times. After Fraedrick opened his second TacoTime restaurant, the task became too much for him to do by hand, so he purchased an electric cement mixer to do the job!

Move Over Denny's

The largest privately owned full service restaurant chain in the Pacific Northwest? That's Shari's! Founded in Hermiston in 1978 and headquartered in Beaverton, its 98 locations serve a half million cups of coffee, a quarter million eggs and five miles of sausage links every year.

EDUCATION

HIGHER EDUCATION

State Colleges
Oregon has seven publicly funded colleges and universities with various bachelor, master and doctorate degree programs. There are also 17 community colleges, 17 independent colleges and universities, three law schools and one state-run medical school.

DID YOU KNOW?

In 2005, 19,138 associate, bachelor, master, doctorate and other degrees were awarded at Oregon's 17 community colleges and eight state-run colleges and universities.

EDUCATION

Bountiful Bachelors

Thirty-one percent of Oregonians have at least a bachelor's degree.

WOW! Is Corvallis Smart!

Between the faculty at Oregon State University, the folks at the local Hewlett Packard plant and all the other bright people in town, Corvallis is one smart city—5.63 percent of its residents have doctoral degrees! Among cities with populations of over 50,000, only three other university towns—Ithaca, New York; Ames, Iowa; and State College, Pennsylvania—have a higher percentage.

They're No Dummies In Portland Either!
A 2004 survey revealed that 37.8 percent of Portland residents 25 years of age or older have at least a bachelor's degree. That makes it the 11th most educated city in the United States!

U.S. News and World Report's **Best Colleges**
Every year, the *U.S. News and World Report* issues its ratings of the best colleges and universities in the United States. A number of Oregon's private institutions ranked high on the 2007 lists. Reed College, Willamette University and Lewis and Clark College were Oregon's best liberal arts colleges. Linfield College was the state's best undergraduate college with a non-liberal arts focus, and the University of Portland, its best university.

Princeton Review's Rankings

Lewis and Clark College, Reed College, University of Oregon and Willamette University made the *Princeton Review*'s list of the "Best of 2007." Lewis and Clark College and Portland State University made the *Princeton Review*'s list of colleges and universities that have excellent community service–learning programs that mix academics with community work

EDUCATION

Best of the West

Eleven of Oregon's institutions of higher learning are on the *Princeton Review*'s "Best of the West" list:

Corban College
George Fox University
Lewis and Clark College
Linfield College
Oregon State University
Pacific University
Portland State University
Reed College
University of Oregon
University of Portland
Willamette University

Want a PhD?
From 1975 to 2004, a higher percentage of Reed College graduates went on to earn doctorates than did the graduates of Harvard, MIT, Stanford and Yale!

Willamette University Firsts

☛ Willamette University was the first institution of higher learning in the western United States. It was established as the Oregon Institute in 1842 to educate missionaries' children in the Willamette Valley.

☛ The university's first building was a three-story structure that students shared with the territorial legislature. For a while, it was the tallest building in the state.

☛ The first medical school in the Pacific Northwest was established at Willamette in 1866. (It's now part of the Oregon Health and Science University). The first law school in the Pacific Northwest was also established there in 1883.

☛ Willamette University was the first co-educational institution in Oregon and one of the first in the country. In fact, its first graduate was a woman: Emily Y. York of the Class of 1859!

EDUCATION

- The first woman to graduate from Willamette's law school was Olive England, Class of 1898, with honors. Women started attending the medical school in 1877.

- Willamette's original name, the Oregon Institute, was changed to "Wallamet University" in 1852 and to its current spelling 18 years later. Took them long enough to pull out the dictionary!

Don't Ever Say Die!
Portland State University started out in 1946 as the Vanport Extension Center to train returning World War II veterans. After the 1948 flood that destroyed Vanport, the center refused to shut its doors, moving instead to downtown Portland in 1952.

It's Big!
With over 35,000 students, Portland State University is Oregon's largest institution of higher learning and is the only public university in Oregon located in a major city. It is also the most racially diverse major university in the Pacific Northwest.

Portland State Alumni
- Phil Knight of Nike fame once taught accounting at Portland State University.

- Jean Aurel, celebrated author of *The Clan of the Cave Bear*, is a graduate.

- Courtney Love, the actress and rock musician, attended Portland State University.

Academic Medicine
The Oregon Health and Science University is the state's only medical school and includes two hospitals, dozens of health clinics and several research centers. With over 11,000 employees, the institution is Portland's largest—and Oregon's fourth largest—corporate employer.

Education in Eastern Oregon
Eastern Oregon University opened in 1929 as a college for women who wanted to be teachers and is the only public university in the state that charges no out-of-state tuition fees.

George Fox University's Famous Faces
George Fox is the only Oregon school of higher learning to have a U.S. president among its alumni. Herbert Hoover attended in 1885–87 when the school was an academy for the children of Oregon's Quaker pioneers and was called the Friends Pacific Academy. Most of the time, Hoover lived off campus with his uncle, Henry John Minthorn (the academy's first principal), and his aunt, Laura Minthorn. But for a few months, Hoover lived in the boy's dormitory that's now known as Minthorn Hall.

Ken Carter, the high school basketball coach who inspired the 2005 movie *Coach Carter*, starring Samuel L. Jackson, is another George Fox alumni.

Mark Hatfield, the first two-term governor of Oregon in the 20th century and a 30-year member of the U.S. Senate, taught one course per term at George Fox University after he retired from politics in 1997.

Technology
The Oregon Institute of Technology is the Pacific Northwest's only accredited public institute of technology and offers degrees in several technology and health-related fields. It opened in 1947 as a vocational school to train World War II veterans.

Oregon State University
Oregon State University opened as the Corvallis Academy in 1856 to provide primary and preparatory education to the local community. It became Corvallis College in 1858 and a state-run agricultural college 10 years after that. The university now offers degrees in over 220 areas of study.

EDUCATION

Civil War Football

Nearly every year since 1894, the Oregon State University Beavers and the University of Oregon Ducks have squared off in one of the oldest football rivalries in America. It's known locally as the "Civil War."

Oregon State University is Tops!

- In 2006, the Carnegie Foundation for the Advancement of Teaching named Oregon State University the state's top research university.

- Only Oregon State University and New York's Cornell University have received space grants, land grants, sea grants and sun grants from the federal government.

- Oregon State University receives more public and private research grant funds every year than Oregon's other six publicly funded colleges and universities combined. In 2004–05, it spent nearly $209 million in research!

- The *U.S. News and World Report* ranked the university's nuclear engineering programs ninth in the country in 2005.

EDUCATION

- Oregon State University's College of Forestry was rated the best in the United States and Canada in 2006.

- In 1999, the university's Valley Library became the first academic library to be named Library of the Year by *The Library Journal*.

Sexy OSU Students

An Oregon State alumnus made history when Jodi Ann Paterson was named *Playboy*'s Playmate of the Year in 2000. The young actress and model is originally from Springfield and was the first Playmate of the Year to have a college degree.

DID YOU  KNOW?

Author Bernard Malamud taught English composition at Oregon State University during the 1940s and '50s. His experiences as a professor were the basis for his 1961 novel, *A New Life*, and it got more than a few tongues wagging on campus. The title of his 1967 Pulitzer Prize winning work, *The Fixer*, was taken from the business sign of a Corvallis bicycle repair store.

Gem in Southern Oregon

The *New York Times* named Southern Oregon University a "hidden gem" of higher education in 2006. The school also appeared in *Outside* magazine's list of best schools for mixing academics with outdoor recreation.

University of Oregon

- The School of Journalism and Communication at the University of Oregon is one of the oldest professional journalism schools in the United States. Established in 1912, eight of its graduates have gone on to win the Pulitzer Prize.

- Stephen Cannell, novelist, screenplay writer and the creator of over 38 TV shows, including *The Rockford Files* and *The A-Team*, is a graduate of the University of Oregon's School of Journalism and Communication.

- University of Oregon's School of Education is ranked 15th in the *U.S. News and World Report*'s list of Best Graduate Schools.

Law at Lewis and Clark

The Northwestern School of Law at Lewis and Clark College started as a state-run law school in Portland in 1884. Twenty-one years later, the Oregon legislature moved the school to Eugene, but the school's administrators and faculty refused to go. The rebels declared their independence, remained in Portland and formed their own private law school, which eventually merged with Lewis and Clark College. And the law school that was transferred to Eugene? It's now the University of Oregon School of Law.

Noted Environmental Law Program

The *U.S. News and World Report* has rated the environmental law program at the Northwestern School of Law at Lewis and Clark College as number one among all such programs in the United States.

Place to Train Future Teachers

One-third of the student body at Western Oregon University is enrolled in the School of Education.

Small Classes and Online Courses

Marylhurst University was the first university in the United States to offer online courses. It was also rated in 2007 by the *U.S. News and World Report* as the best college or university in the Pacific Northwest in terms of small class size.

EDUCATION

From Orphan School To University
Pacific University started in 1842 as a school for Native American orphans. It became a combination academy and college 12 years later and continued to offer high school as well as university courses until 1915.

The 411 on the 4-1-4
Linfield is one of the few colleges in the United States to offer a 4-1-4 academic calendar. It consists of fall and spring semesters as well as an optional four-week intensive study term in January. Students complete a full semester course in just four weeks! Often students take this opportunity to enroll in a course that is a little out of the ordinary, become an intern or study abroad.

DID YOU KNOW?

Corban College was known as Western Baptist College until 2005.

EDUCATION

ELEMENTARY AND SECONDARY EDUCATION

The Statistics

During the 2005–06 school year, 559,244 youngsters enrolled from pre-kindergarten through grade 12 in 1282 public schools across Oregon. This includes the 7586 who enrolled in public charter schools. Another 41,000 K–12 students are enrolled in private school. There are 18,000 homeschooled children.

Student Body Population Growth

Over the last decade and a half, the number of students attending Oregon's public schools has increased by 9.6 percent.

Student Diversity

The racial or ethnic identity of Oregon's students has gone through major changes in the last 15 years.

	1992–93 (%)	2005–06 (%)
White	87.5	71.7
African American	2.4	3.0
American Hispanic	5.3	15.1
Asian/Pacific Islander	3.0	4.5
Native American	1.8	2.1
Multi-Race or Multi-Ethnic	n/a	1.1
Not Reported	n/a	2.5

DID YOU  KNOW?

The percentage of students from ethnic minorities who graduate from high school or earn a GED has risen from 63 percent in 1994 to 76 percent in 2006.

Languages Spoken at School

English is not the primary language for 11.7 percent of Oregon's students. These young people speak 137 other languages. By far, the most common is Spanish, which is spoken by 76.9 percent of them. The five most common languages after Spanish and English are:

Russian	5.5 percent
Vietnamese	3.0 percent
Ukrainian	1.5 percent
Korean	1.1 percent
Cantonese or Yue	1.0 percent

EDUCATION

ESL

As of 2004, 40 percent or more of the students in the Woodburn, Jefferson County, Nyssa, Gervais and Umatilla schools districts are enrolled in English as a Second Language programs. In Woodburn and Jefferson Counties more than half of the students participate in these programs!

DID YOU  KNOW?

In 2005–06, 42.7 percent of the students attending Oregon's K–12 public schools were eligible for free or reduced-price lunches. Typically, the younger the students, the higher the percentage of those who qualify for the program.

School's Out?
Of all the students enrolled in Oregon's K–12 public schools, 13,159 are homeless.

The Breakdown: Schools
Oregon has 710 elementary schools, 170 middle schools, 30 junior high schools, 24 combined schools and 219 high schools. There is one school for the blind and one for the deaf.

How Many People Does It Take to Educate 560,000 Students?

In the 2005–06 school year, Oregon's 198 school districts and related institutions employed 27,301 teachers, 9344 educational aides, 521 curriculum specialists, 1246 counselors, 1220 librarians and media specialists and 2322 administrators as well as 4572 administrative support staff, 1879 other professionals and 8358 others who help keep the schools going. That's more than 57,000 people!

EDUCATION

The Teachers (2005–06)

☞ The average number of years of experience of an Oregon public school teacher: 12.9

☞ The average age of an Oregon teacher: 44 years

☞ The median age: 54 years

☞ The average annual salary of an Oregon public school teacher: $49,839. If you adjust this salary for inflation, it's one percent lower than a teacher's salary in 1992–93.

A Well-Educated Group of Teachers

☞ 69.4 percent of all Oregon teachers, and 85.0 percent of the state's elementary school teachers, are women.

☞ 56.7 percent of Oregon's public school teachers have master's degrees. Only 33 percent of the public school teachers in California have master's degrees. In Idaho, only 24.4 percent do.

☞ 0.3 percent have doctorates.

☞ 32.6 percent of Oregon's public school teachers have taken college courses beyond their bachelor's degrees.

☞ 66 percent of Oregon's grade 7–12 students are taught by instructors who have undergraduate or graduate degrees in the field they are teaching.

How Big Are Those School Districts?

☞ Of Oregon's 198 school districts, 107 have fewer than 1000 students. Together, these 107 districts serve only 6.6 percent students.

☞ Seventeen districts have 7000 or more pupils! The five largest serve 28.9 percent of the K–12 students. They are in Portland, Salem, Beaverton, Eugene and Hillsboro.

EDUCATION

How Much Does It Cost to Educate All Those Students?

	Total (in billions)	Per Student
2001–02	$4413.3	$7756
2002–03	$4237.9	$7571
2003–04	$4706.6	$7760
2004–05	$4642.5	$8200

DID YOU  KNOW?

The average school building in Oregon is over 40 years old!

Source of Funding

Throughout most of Oregon's history, the public schools were financed by local property taxes. Measure 5, the property tax limitation law approved by the voters in 1990, changed all that.

	1989–1990 (%)	2004–05 (%)
Local Money	66.8	33.3
State Money	25.5	52.4
Federal Money	5.9	10.9
Intermediate and other sources	1.8	3.3

That's a Lot of Cap and Gowns!

In 2004–05, 36,538 students completed high school in Oregon; 32,350 of them received a regular diploma, and a record

EDUCATION

32.8 percent graduated with a Certificate of Initial Mastery (CIM). The CIM indicates that the student met all of the state's requirements in math, public speaking, reading, science and writing.

DID YOU  KNOW?

Seventy-nine percent of Oregon's adults between the ages of 18 and 24 have a high school diploma. Another nine percent have a General Education Development credential. That's one of the highest percentages of young adults with GEDs in the United States and one point higher than the national average.

Dropout Rate Down

While the number of students in grades 9 through 12 in Oregon's schools has increased since the 1997–98 school year, the dropout rate has gone down.

Students		Dropouts	Rate	Percent
1997–98		159,121	10,947	6.9
1998–99		161,263	10,622	6.6
1999–2000		164,554	10,363	6.3
2000–01		166,039	8713	5.2
2001–02		167,975	8160	4.9
2002–03		170,424	7439	4.4
2003–04	171,732		7864	4.6
2004–05	175,501		7318	4.2

The biggest decrease in the dropout rate between 2003–04 and 2004–05 was among Hispanic students (from 9.6 percent to 8.1 percent) and African American students (from 8.2 percent to 6.0 percent). However, 21 percent of all 9–12 graders who dropped out in 2004–05 were Hispanic. Only 3.5 percent of the white grade 9–12 students dropped out in 2004–05.

Ready for College?

Among the 23 states where at least 50 percent of the graduating class participated in the Scholastic Assessment Test (SAT) in 2006, Oregon ranked second on both the math and verbal sections. The state ranked fifth on the writing section.

College Bound?

The percentage of Oregon high school graduates who were enrolled in a two-year or a four-year college or university in the fall immediately after their graduation has steadily increased since 1993. Typically, more women than men enter college. In 2005, 69.4 percent of high school graduates began college in the fall. It is estimated that at least another 20 percent will begin attending college sometime after that.

College Dropout Rate

Only 55 percent of Oregon's full-time undergraduate students earn a bachelor's degree within six years. Furthermore, while 76 percent of freshmen at Oregon's four-year colleges and universities come back to the same institution for their sophomore year, only 44 percent of Oregon's first year community college students return for their second year of studies.

DID YOU KNOW?

If all Oregonians had the same level of education and earnings as its white population, then the total personal income in the state would increase by $1.5 billion.

EDUCATION

HIGHER ED QUICK FACTS

Staying in School

There were 199,985 college students in Oregon in 2004. These included:

Undergraduates	174,619
Graduate students	20,589
Professional students	4777

Of these, 122,191 of these students were full-time, and 77,794 were part-time.

Public vs. Private

Here are the numbers for post-secondary students attending public and private colleges:

- 65,816 attend public four-year institutions
- 82,860 attend public two-year institutions
- 23,396 attend private four-year institutions
- 2547 attend private two-year institutions

DID YOU KNOW?

Sixteen percent of Oregon's high school graduates and 37.7 percent of those with GPAs of 3.75 or better will attend an out-of-state college or university.

EDUCATION

Tuition

The average tuition in 2005–06 for a full-time student at one of Oregon's community colleges was $2642 a year. The average tuition for a full-time student at a state-run four-year college or university was $5345 a year. The average tuition at a private college or university was $20,952!

How Do Students Pay for College?
Of those 2005 Oregon high school graduates that went on to college:

- 37.7 percent received one or more scholarships
- 36.0 percent received student loans
- 23.0 percent were offered Pell grants
- 16.2 percent were receiving college work-study funding

Of course, many students received funds from more than one of these sources.

POLITICS

PRESIDENTIAL POLITICS

Two presidents lived in the Beaver State before moving into the White House.

Ulysses S. Grant lived at Fort Vancouver, near present-day Vancouver, Washington, from 1852 to 1853. Since Washington was then still part of the Oregon Territory, Grant was, technically, an Oregonian!

Nearly 40 years later, Herbert Hoover spent part of his childhood and teenage years in Newberg living with his uncle and aunt.

Oregon voted once in favor, and once against, each of its adopted sons. Each time it voted against them, that state cast its vote for a New Yorker: Horatio Seymour in 1868 and Franklin Roosevelt in 1932.

DID YOU  KNOW?

In 1868, Grant was elected president, when he was only 46 years old. Until Theodore Roosevelt reached the White House in 1901 at the tender age of 42, Grant was the youngest president in history.

Hoover in Newberg

Although he was born in Iowa in 1874, Herbert Hoover lived in Newberg from 1884 to 1891 with his uncle and aunt, John and Laura Minthorn, who were the administrators of present-day George Fox College. While there, Hoover briefly attended the Friends Pacific Academy (as George Fox was then known) and worked as an office boy in his uncle's Oregon Land Company real estate office in Salem. Hoover left Oregon for Stanford University in 1891 to earn a degree in geology.

The house where Hoover resided while he lived in Newberg is now a museum. The furniture in his former bedroom is the actual set used by the president as a boy.

DID YOU  KNOW?

Hoover died in 1964 at the age of 90. Until Gerald Ford, he was the oldest former president in American history.

Presidential Nominee and Hero!
The presidential nominee of the Socialist Labor Party in 1928 was Frank T. Johns of Portland. On May 21 of that year, while giving a speech in Bend, he heard the cries of a young boy who had fallen into the Deschutes River. He immediately jumped off the podium and into the river to save the young lad. Unfortunately, the rescue was unsuccessful, and they both drowned.

POLITICS

Oregonians for Vice President

Two Oregonians have been nominated as vice president. In 1860, the year that Republican Abraham Lincoln was sent to the White House, the Democrats were bitterly divided, and the two factions each nominated their own candidates for president and vice president. The first territorial governor of Oregon, Joseph Lane, was one of the vice-presidential nominees.

In 1940, when Democrat Franklin Roosevelt was running for reelection, the Republicans nominated U.S. Senator Charles McNary of Oregon for vice president. Ironically, Oregon voted for neither of their native vice-presidential candidates.

During the 1972 presidential election, a Republican elector from Virginia was so upset by the Watergate scandal that he cast his ballot for the Libertarian candidates. Theodora Nathan, the Libertarian's vice presidential nominee, was from Eugene and was the first woman in American history to receive a vote in the Electoral College.

A Close One!
The closest presidential election in Oregon in the last 100 years was the 1976 campaign. With over one million votes cast, Gerald Ford defeated Jimmy Carter by a mere 1713 votes! Only in Ohio was the election any closer that year.

The 2000 election between Al Gore and George W. Bush was another squeaker. With 1.5 million votes cast, only 6765 votes separated the candidates.

POLITICS

BLUE VS. RED

Democrats and Republicans

Just like the rest of the country, the proportion of Democratic and Republican voters is not evenly distributed across Oregon. Democrats are concentrated in the highly urbanized areas where one out of every five Oregon voters live. Republican voters are concentrated in the rural areas east of the Cascade Mountains and south of Eugene. The rest of the state swings based on the election.

DID YOU  KNOW?

Over 40 percent of the votes cast in Oregon are by voters living in Clackamas, Multnomah or Washington counties. This concentration of voters can produce some interesting election results. In 2004, for example, John Kerry won 51.35 percent of the statewide vote, but carried only eight of the state's 36 counties.

POLITICS

How Politically Liberal or Conservative Are You?

The non-partisan Bay Area Center for Voting Research recently ranked 237 American cities with a population of over 100,000 from most to least liberal. Detroit, Michigan, was ranked as the country's most liberal city and Provo, Utah, as the most conservative. Three Oregon cities were included in the study. Portland ranked 29th most liberal and Eugene ranked 54th. Salem was far behind: at 140th on the liberal-leaning list, it was the 98th most conservative city studied.

A Good Example of Civic Responsibility!
According to the federal government's Election Assistance Commission, 71.4 percent of Oregonians who were eligible to vote in 2004 did. That's the fifth highest rate in the country. The national average is only 60.9 percent.

The rate of registered voters who cast a ballot was even higher. At 86.5 percent, only Minnesota, Wyoming and Connecticut had a higher voter turnouts, than Oregon. And in 2004, 82.5 percent of those in Oregon who were eligible to vote were registered to vote.

Don't Forget to Lick the Stamp!

Unlike the residents of the other 49 states, Oregonians don't go into a voting booth on Election Day. Instead, they cast their ballots by mail!

Voting by mail on a limited basis was approved by the state legislature in 1981 and was made permanent in 1987. In 1998, the state went even further. By a more than a two to one margin, Oregon voters made vote-by-mail the only way to cast a ballot in the primary and general elections of even-numbered years beginning in 2000.

More than Just the Democrats and the Republicans!

Aside from the Democrats and the Republicans, there are four other statewide political parties in Oregon: the Constitution Party, the Libertarian Party, the Pacific Green Party and the Working Families Party. In the Third Congressional District, there is also a Socialist Party. Other political parties that have been on the ballot in Oregon over the years include:

Communists
Constitutional Unionists
Greenbacks
Independent Initiative Party
Industrial Labor Party
Liberal Republicans
National Labor Reformers
Natural Law Party
New Alliance Party
People's Party

Progressives
Prohibitionists
Regular People's Party
National Gold Democrats
Silver Republicans
Social Democrats
Socialists
Socialist Labor Party
United Labor Party
U.S. Taxpayers Party

Independents often run in Oregon, and some have been elected. One independent, Julius Meier, became governor in 1930.

Dorchester

Oregon politics is famous for the Dorchester Conference, an annual get-together where state Republicans meet candidates, debate issues and discuss policy and strategy. Founded in 1964 by a young politician named Bob Packwood, the conference was intended as a forum for liberal Republicans. By the 1990s, however, the conference was dominated by party conservatives.

Nader's Success

When Ralph Nader "stood" for president in 1996—he did not campaign, and he spent less than $5000—he received 3.59 percent of Oregon's total vote. That was Nader's best showing in the country that year.

When Nader campaigned for president in 2000, he received 5.04 percent of Oregon's vote, far less than the 10 percent he won in Alaska.

Oregon: Democrat or Republican?
Before 1986, Oregon cast its vote for the GOP ticket in 25 of the 32 presidential elections. Republicans won 20 of the 34 gubernatorial elections during the same period. Since 1986, however, Oregon has elected only Democratic governors and has voted for every Democratic presidential nominee.

However, these facts can be deceiving. Consider:

- Twenty-five percent of Oregon voters are registered with a minor political party or as independents.

- One or both of Oregon's U.S. senators since 1967 has been a Republican.

- Although every governor for the past 20 years has been a Democrat, the Republicans were in control of the Oregon Senate from 1995 to 2001 and of the Oregon House of Representatives from 1991 to 2007.

TRANSPORTATION

HIGHWAYS AND DRIVING HABITS

Highways of All Sorts
Believe it or not, Route 501 is the same road as Alsea-Deadwood Highway 201. Why? Many roads in Oregon have two names, one given by the Oregon Department of Transportation and another derived from the U.S. Route system. To the uninitiated, it can be very confusing indeed!

Get Oregon Out of the Mud!
To generate support for its building projects, the Oregon Department of Transportation uses slogans. The best of the past 100 years are:

- "Get Oregon Out of the Mud" (1913)
- "Building Oregon Thru Better Highways" (1957)
- "Oregon Freeways…Symbol of 2nd Century Progress" (1958)
- "Freeways are Easier" (1961)
- "Fifty Years of Building Better Highways in Oregon" (1967)
- "Keep Oregon Green and in the Black" (1978)
- "ODOT on the Move" (1986)
- "Celebrate the interstate!" (2006)

No Self-Serve
It's illegal for motorists in Oregon to pump their own gas and has been since 1951. (New Jersey is the only other state with such a law.) A measure to remove the ban was put on the ballot in 1982, but Oregonians voted it down. It's okay for motorcyclists to fill up their bikes with gasoline.

TRANSPORTATION

A Highway First
Built between Astoria and The Dalles from 1913 to 1922, the 196-mile Columbia River Highway was the first modern highway in the Pacific Northwest. It was also the country's first scenic highway.

To promote tourism, 74 miles of the original highway has recently been designated the Historic Columbia River Highway. Forty of those miles are open to cars, while the rest will be turned into bicycle and hiking trails as soon as money becomes available. Sites along the highway, such as the Moser Tunnels, are also being restored.

That's Short!
The shortest state highway in the Beaver State is Oregon Route 70 between Dairy and Bonanza. It's only seven miles long! Locals know it as the Dairy-Bonanza Highway.

DID YOU  KNOW?

Oregon drivers can enjoy two scenic roads that are on the American Automobile Association's "10 Most Beautiful List" without ever leaving the state. One is the 33-mile Rim Drive that circles Crater Lake. The other is the Columbia River Gorge Highway from Troutdale to Boardman.

The State of Jefferson
While most of it is in California, about 15 miles of the State of Jefferson Scenic Byway is in Oregon. Better known as California State Highway 96 and U.S. Forest Service Primary Route 48, the byway connects the small community of O'Brien with Yreka, California. But where (or what) is the State of Jefferson?

The byway's name is in remembrance of an attempt in 1941 by Port Orford mayor, Gilbert Gable, and others to create a new state out of Curry, Jackson, Josephine and Klamath counties as well as Del Norte, Modoc and Siskiyou counties in California. Seems they were unhappy with the condition of the local roads and tired of Oregon and California doing nothing about it. They got as far as having a provisional governor inaugurated and a provisional capital established in Yreka, but then the whole idea was forgotten when Pearl Harbor was attacked and the United States entered World War II.

Auto Accidents

Oregon's auto accident fatality rate is 13.9 deaths per 100,000 residents. The state's most densely populated counties, Multnomah and Washington, have the lowest auto fatality rates.

DID YOU KNOW?

Oregonians drive 9900 miles per year per resident and use, on average, eight gallons of gasoline per week.

How Do We Get to Work?

According to the 2000 census, 1.6 million Oregonians go to work every day. Of those:

- 73.2 percent drive to work alone
- 12.2 percent carpool
- 4.2 percent take transit
- 3.6 percent walk
- 1.9 percent get to work by other means
- 5.0 percent work at home

CELEBRITIES

HOLLYWOOD IN OREGON

DID YOU KNOW?

The earliest movie known to be filmed in Oregon was a 30-second silent short called *Fast Money, Northern Pacific Railroad*. It was shot near Portland in 1897. Buster Keaton's *The General* (1927) was the first full-length movie filmed in the state.

Native Son

Oregon filmmaker Gus Van Sant has shot many of his films in the state, among them are:
  Drugstore Cowboy (1989)
  Elephant (2003)
  Even Cowgirls Get the Blues (1993)
  My Own Private Idaho (1991)

Movie Mecca
Over 600 movies and documentaries were partially or entirely shot in Oregon. Among the most famous are:

- 1941 (1979)
- Abe Lincoln in Illinois (1940)
- Animal House (1978)
- The Apple Dumpling Gang (1975)
- Artificial Intelligence: A. I. (2001)
- Bandits (2001)
- The Black Stallion (1979)
- Bronco Billy (1980)
- Dead Man (1995)
- Elizabethtown (2005)
- Five Easy Pieces (1970)
- The Goonies (1985)
- Independence Day (1996)
- Kindergarten Cop (1990)
- Maverick (1994)
- Mr. Holland's Opus (1995)
- My Name is Bruce (2007)
- Northwest Passage (1940)
- One Flew Over the Cuckoo's Nest (1975)
- Paint Your Wagon (1969)
- Point Break (1991)
- The Ring (2002)
- The Ring Two (2005)
- Rooster Cogburn (1975)
- Shenandoah (1965)
- The Shining (1980)
- Short Circuit (1986)
- Sometimes a Great Notion (1971)
- Stand by Me (1986)

Movie Magic?!?
Paul Newman and Robert Redford famously jump off a cliff into a river near Merlin in *Butch Cassidy and the Sundance Kid* (1969).

That's Censorship!
The 1967 movie, *The Graduate*, was originally suppose to be filmed at the University of Oregon, but Arthur Fleming, the president of UO, denied permission because he didn't like the script.

Television Comes to Oregon
Episodes from several television shows have also been filmed in Oregon, including *Cops, Gunsmoke, Oregon Kara Ai (From Oregon with Love), Route 66* and *Have Gun, Will Travel*.

CELEBRITIES

THE PRESS AND PULITZERS

The Old Giant of Oregon Newspapers

There are over 90 newspapers published in Oregon, but by far the largest is Portland's *The Oregonian*. Over 320,000 copies are distributed across the state every weekday and over 380,000 on Sundays. By way of contrast, Eugene's *Register-Guard* has a daily circulation of 70,000, a Saturday circulation of 79,000 and a Sunday circulation of 75,000. Founded in 1850, *The Oregonian* is also the oldest continuously published newspaper on the West Coast.

The Pulitzer Prize and *The Oregonian*

Seven Pulitzer Prizes have been awarded to Oregon newspapers and their staff. Five of those prizes were shared by *The Oregonian* and its staff. The five winners were:

- Associate Editor Ronald Callvert who was awarded the Pulitzer Prize for Editorial Writing in 1939 for a year of exemplarily editorial reporting. His piece "My County 'Tis of Thee" was specifically mentioned as an example of his wonderful work. Callvert is also the author of "Sings a Song to America" which is considered one of the greatest news-paper editorials ever written.

- Staff reporters Wallace Turner and William Lambert won a Pulitzer for Local Reporting in 1957 for their exposé of corruption and vice involving Portland officials and the Teamsters.

- Staff reporter Richard Read won the Pulitzer Prize for Explanatory Reporting in 1999 for a series he entitled *The French Fry Connection*. In the series, Read illustrated the effects of the Asian economic crisis of the late 1990s upon America by focusing on its impact on Oregon's local french fry industry.

- *The Oregonian* as a whole won the Pulitzer Prize for Public Service in 2001 for its detailed and critical examination of the abuse of foreign nationals and other problems within the U.S. Immigration and Naturalization Service.

- Staff writer Tom Hallman Jr., won a Pulitzer for Feature Writing in 2001 for his series *The Boy Behind the Mask*. The subject of Hallman's reporting was a teen with a facial deformity.

Other Prize-Winning Papers

The Oregonian has not monopolized the Pulitzer. Medford's *Mail Tribune* received the Pulitzer Prize for Public Service in 1934 for its reporting of the efforts of Medford businessmen and fascists Llewellyn Banks and Earl Fehl to take over Jackson County in 1932–33. The men and their supporters threatened and harassed businessmen, politicians and anyone else who opposed them. In 1932, 10,000 ballots were stolen to prevent a recount of the 1932 election in which Fehl was elected county sheriff. A police officer was eventually murdered. In the end, Banks went to prison and Fehl lost his job and was declared insane.

Nigel Jaquiss of Portland's *Willamette Week* won a Pulitzer for Investigative Reporting in 2005 for his online article exposing former Oregon Governor Neil Goldschmidt's three-year sexual relationship with a 14-year-old girl while Goldschmidt was mayor of Portland during the 1970s. This was the first time that the Pulitzer was awarded for a story that first appeared on a newspaper's website.

CELEBRITIES

SOME NOTABLE OREGONIANS

Famous Cartoonist Cut From High School Paper!
Matt Groening, of *The Simpsons* fame, was born in Portland in 1954 and attended Lincoln High School. In the eyes of his family, he was a success from day one. His father—named Homer!—was a cartoonist himself and knew Matt had talent. But Matt's peers didn't share that enthusiasm and cut him from the staff of his high school paper.

Following graduation, Matt was Hollywood bound. His car broke down in the middle of the Hollywood Freeway, and he was initially stuck working as the chauffer for an 88-year-old movie director. But Matt turned these experiences into an underground comic strip entitled *Life in Hell*. The strip was a huge success and is currently syndicated in 250 newspapers worldwide. It also caught the attention of producer James L. Brooks, who hired him to do some animation. Brooks' assignment inadvertently resulted in *The Simpsons*, which debuted on Fox in 1990 and has become the longest-running prime-time animated show in history.

DID YOU  KNOW?

The Simpsons have the same names as the members of Matt Groening's family. Except for Bart—his name is an anagram of brat. Flanders, Lovejoy, Powell, Quimby and Terwilliger are all Portland street names.

Class Clowns?
Matt Groening and Mel Blanc (the actor behind the voices of Bugs Bunny, Daffy Duck and Porky Pig) went to the same Portland high school. Groening was a member of the Class of 1973 and Blanc the Class of 1941.

Renowned Author

Born in McMinnville in 1916, Beverly Atlee Bunn, a.k.a. Beverly Cleary, was in her 30s before making a name for herself in the world of children's literature. With a background in library studies, her solid knowledge of the genre gave her the backing she needed to produce 30 books. Altogether her books have sold more than 10 million copies.

Fancy Footwork

Ginger Rogers, one half of Hollywood's greatest dancing duo, chose Oregon as her home for more than 50 years. Born in Independence, Missouri, in 1911, Virginia "Ginger" McMath won a four-week vaudeville contract at the age of 14. In 1933, when she was paired with Fred Astaire in *Flying Down to Rio,* her career really took off. The duo made a total of nine hit musical films together, and Ginger also acted in several independent roles, earning an Academy Award in the process.

Eventually, she bought a 1000-acre ranch near Eagle Point, Oregon, in an effort to create a distance between her public and her very private life. She died in 1995.

DID YOU KNOW?

Kim Novak (*Vertigo*) is another Hollywood star who made Eagle Point her home.

More Famous Oregonians

- Musician Doc Severinsen, best known as the leader of the NBC Orchestra on Johnny Carson's *The Tonight Show*, was born in Arlington.

- The mother of Academy Award–winner William Hurt is from Burns.

- Ken Kesey, author of *One Flew Over the Cuckoo's Nest*, spent most of the last 30 years of his life in Pleasant Hill.

- Academy Award–winner Clark Gable worked for a lumber company in Bend, sold ties in Portland, helped build a logging road near Silverton and toured with an acting company in Astoria and Seaside before taking acting lessons in Portland and making it big.

- Carl Barks, the cartoonist who created Donald Duck and several other characters, was born in Merrill, grew up in Midland, and after a long and successful career, retired to Grants Pass.

- Bruce Campbell, the star of such comedy-horror cult movie classics as *The Army of Darkness* and *Bubba Ho-Tep*, lives in Jacksonville.

- Vance Colvig, the original Bozo the Clown and the voice of such Disney characters as Goofy, Grumpy and Pluto, was born in Jacksonville.

- Western actor Jack Elam (*Support Your Local Sheriff*) lived in Ashland after he retired from the movies.

- Actor Danny Glover owns a house in Dunthorpe.

- Actor River Phoenix (*My Own Private Idaho*) was born in Madras, and his director, Gus Van Sant, lives in Portland.

- Folk musician and composer Tim Hardin was born in Eugene.

SPORTS HEROES

Medals for Oregonians

Since 1906, 64 Oregonians have brought home 81 Olympic medals. Of those, 42 have been gold! Bert Kerrigan, Oregon's first Olympian, earned a bronze medal for high jump in 1906. Oregon's first multiple medal winner, Norman Ross, brought back three gold medals for swimming from the 1920 Summer Olympics in Antwerp.

The 1984 Olympics proved to be Oregon's most prolific, with eight medals won that year.

DID YOU KNOW?

Oregon's only Heisman Trophy winner was Oregon State University quarterback Terry Baker who won the award in 1962. During his last year with the Beavers, he led in total offense with 2276 yards. He also had a career total of 4980 yards of running and passing. A multi-talented athlete, Baker came to the school on a basketball scholarship and was part of the university's basketball team when it made NCAA tournament appearances in 1961–62 and in 1962–63.

The Portland Trail Blazers

The Trail Blazers are the only major league professional basketball team in the state. They entered the National Basketball Association as an expansion team in 1970 and won the NBA Championship seven years later. They were proclaimed the state team in 1991.

Hall of Fame

Oregon has an impressive athletic history, and the Oregon Sports Hall of Fame has been honoring the best of the state's athletes since 1980. Over 200 men and women in over 25 individual events, as well as coaches and sports broadcasters, have been inducted into the Hall of Fame since 1980. Most of the inductees have played football, basketball, track and field, baseball, golf, swimming and diving. But there have also been athletes from sports as diverse as auto racing, fencing, duathlon, soccer, handball, rodeo, volleyball and trap shooting.

2006 Inductees to the Oregon Sports Hall of Fame

Judy Bochenski	Table Tennis
Terry Brandon	Basketball
Doug LaMear	Broadcasting
Roy Love	Coaching
Wayne Twitchell	Baseball

OUTDOOR FUN

Downhill Skiing

Oregon has many excellent ski hills and people travel from around the world to take advantage of them. And with good reason. Not only are the views spectacular, resorts such as the Timberline and Mount Bachelor ski areas are often open most of the year.

Oregon Adaptive Sports

Founded in 1996 as the Oregon Adaptive Skiing Program, Oregon Adaptive Sports helps people with disabilities enjoy downhill skiing. The non-profit organization provides special ski equipment, and volunteers train participants to use it on the slopes. There are enough volunteers and equipment to provide 350 ski sessions each year.

Oregon Marathons

Four marathons are held each year in Newport, Portland, Bend and Eugene. They're all 26.2 miles long each one has its own special charm.

Newport Marathon

In 2004, Herb Phillips of Burnaby, BC, ran the marathon in 2:47:28. That was fast enough to break the single age World Record for 63-year-old males.

Runners are offered Yaquina Bay Oyster "shooters" at miles 11 and 19. According to race organizers, one runner in 2006 ate 43!

Portland Marathon

This race prides itself on being walker-friendly. Its course remains open for eight hours, allowing everyone to finish at their own pace. Every year since 1998, more than half of the marathon's finishers have been women.

Haulin Aspen Trail Marathon, Bend
Runners in this scenic race catch sights of Mount Bachelor, Tumalo Mountain and sometimes even Broken Top and the Sisters. Ninety-nine percent of this race is run on dirt surfaces.

Eugene Marathon
This is a marathon event with something for everyone. In addition to the 26-mile race, there is a half marathon, a 5K run and a 1-mile kids' run. A nine-week kids marathon lets groups of kids run 26.2 miles bit by bit to raise money for charities or for their schools.

DID YOU  KNOW?

Interested in swimming and biking before running your mini-marathon? Well, in Oregon, there is at least one triathlon scheduled every week during the summer months.

Sled Dog Race
Want to participate in an Iditarod, but can't make it to Alaska or the Yukon? Then try the Eagle Cap Sled Dog Race in Joseph! Every January, mushers and their canine companions try their luck on one of two courses. The first is a 100-mile race for eight-dog teams, and the other is twice as long for 12-dog teams. The event is often called "Oregon's Iditarod" and the "Toughest Race in the Northwest," and it is an official qualifier for both the famous Alaska Iditarod and for the Yukon's Quest sled dog races.

SCIENCE AND TECHNOLOGY

INVENTIONS AND GADGETS

The Screwdriver
Ever hear of Portland's Henry Phillips? No. Then how about the Phillips head screwdriver? He invented it. His design was so widely copied that he lost the patent to his invention in 1949.

Of Mice and Worldwide Webs
Douglas C. Engelbart's life began near Portland in 1925; he attended Oregon State University and earned a PhD in electrical engineering from the University of California at Berkeley in 1955. As a member of the Stanford Research Institute, he invented the precursor to today's computer mouse and, with his colleagues, introduced video conferencing, teleconferencing, e-mail, hypertext and other innovations to the world. He was recognized for his efforts with numerous prizes and honors, including the $500,000 Lemelson-MIT Prize in 1997 and the National Medal of Technology in 2000.

The Importance of Play
He may have earned a degree in medicine, but Salem-born Alfred Carlton Gilbert wasn't about to use his knowledge in the conventional way. As a youth, Gilbert is reported to have run off to join a minstrel show. He was about 20 miles away from home before his father finally caught up with him. Athletically strong, he earned an Olympic gold medal in 1908 in the pole vault.

Gilbert and a business partner formed the Mysto-Manufacturing Company in 1909. Within a few years the toy company had grown from making magic sets to building girder-based erector sets. By 1935, more than 30 million of the famous Erector Sets had been sold! The company also developed several chemistry and microscope sets. Gilbert died in 1961. A children's museum, called A.C. Gilbert's Discovery Village, is in Salem.

SCIENCE AND TECHNOLOGY

DID YOU  KNOW?

In 1918, with the United States fighting World War I, the federal government considered banning the production of toys so more factories would produce war material. Gilbert fought the move, won and was labeled by the press as the "Man Who Saved Christmas." There's even a 2002 movie by that name about Gilbert's efforts to save the holiday.

Did You Also Know?
Alfred Gilbert paid his way through Yale by working as a magician.

Ballooning to Oregon?

Back in 1849 everyone was making his or her way out west, and Rufus Porter, the founder of *Scientific American* magazine, wanted to make the voyage easier. He thought air travel was a wonderful alternative to trekking over mountains and forging across rivers. So, he devised an idea to use hot air balloons equipped with steam engines to propel diehard adventurers to their new homes in Oregon. Close to 200 people were willing give his idea a try. Lucky for them, the idea never turned into reality.

SCIENCE AND TECHNOLOGY

NOBEL PRIZE WINNERS

Oregon's Nobel Laureates

Three Oregonians have won the Nobel Prize. William P. Murphy won it for medicine in 1934. Linus Pauling won the prize for chemistry in 1954 and for peace in 1962, making him the only person in history to win two unshared Nobel Prizes. In 2001, Carl Wieman won the prize in physics.

William P. Murphy

University of Oregon alumnus William P. Murphy taught high school math and physics for a few years and then worked as a medical laboratory assistant at the U of O before earning a medical degree at Harvard. He then briefly practiced medicine before joining the faculty at Harvard where he taught for 40 years.

Murphy was particularly interested in the diseases of the blood, and this led to his research on how to treat pernicious anemia. This severe disease is characterized not only by the lack of red blood corpuscles but also by the production of antibodies that attack the nerve cells in the stomach. Murphy bled dogs to make them anemic and then fed them various things to see if they improved. Once he discovered that large amounts of liver cured the disease, Murphy's fellow scientists went about to find out why. George Richards Minot and George Hoyt Whipple eventually determined that a deficiency of vitamin B-12 caused pernicious anemia and that liver and other sources of B-12 were the cure. For their efforts, all three shared the 1934 Nobel Prize in medicine.

Linus Pauling

The world's greatest chemist during the 20th century was, without a doubt, Oregon's Linus Pauling. Interested in chemistry since he was a lad, the Portland native was admitted to the Oregon Agricultural College in Corvallis (now Oregon State University) at the age of 16. Pauling joined the college's faculty as a full-time instructor of quantitative analysis while he was still only an 18-year-old student. After receiving his bachelor's degree, Pauling continued his studies at the California Institute of Technology and was awarded a PhD at the tender age of 24. He immediately became a professor at Caltech and remained there until his death 60 years later.

Since his teenage years, Pauling was particularly interested in molecular structures and the nature of the chemical bonds between these infinitesimally small bodies. His research and many discoveries reshaped the science of chemistry and led to his award of the Nobel Prize in chemistry in 1954. He was also interested in biochemistry, made significant contributions toward discovering a treatment for sickle cell anemia, and was well on his way to discovering the double helix of DNA when Francis Crick and James Watson beat him to it in 1953.

The horrors of World War II turned Pauling into a pacifist and peace activist. Indeed, his politics led the State Department to deny him a passport to prevent him from traveling overseas. (Pauling's passport was restored in 1954, just in time for him to go to Sweden to receive his Nobel Prize.) Pauling's efforts played a key role in creating the public pressure that lead to the Nuclear Test Ban Treaty in 1963. For his work, Pauling was awarded the 1962 Nobel Peace Prize. However, it was the middle of the Cold War, and many saw Pauling as nothing but a naïve stooge for the communists. *Life* magazine called his award an "insult," and he was forced to defend himself in front of a Senate committee. Even his own chemistry department at Caltech refused to congratulate him on winning the peace prize.

Pauling Quick Facts

- Pauling was diagnosed with Bright's disease at the age of 40. The disease is usually fatal, but a low-protein, salt-free diet supplemented with vitamins and minerals allowed him to live for another 54 years. The experience made him an advocate of alternative medicine.

- Linus Pauling received 47 honorary doctorates.

- At the age of 61, he also received an honorary high school diploma from his alma mater, Washington High School in Portland. The greatest chemist of his age had, ironically, never graduated from high school because he had neglected to take some required courses in American history.

- At age 32, Pauling became the youngest person in history to be admitted to the National Academy of Sciences.

- Pauling's work in alternative medicine eventually led him to advocate high doses of vitamin C to fight cancer. Most of what Pauling said was dismissed as quackery, but recent medical research indicates that he may have been right.

- Since 1996, the Linus Pauling Institute at Oregon State University has been a major center of research into how vitamins, minerals and other nutrients can help fight aging, cancer, heart disease and diseases that attack the nervous system.

Carl Wieman

Born and raised in Corvallis, Carl Wieman was educated at the Massachusetts Institute of Technology and Stanford University before he received a teaching job at the University of Colorado. While at UC, he was part of a team in 1995 that created the first true Bose-Einstein condensate in history. The condensate was a new form of matter created when really tiny particles, known as bosons, are supercooled to absolute zero. That's −460°F!

A FEW LAST WORDS

TOP TEN REASONS TO LIVE IN OREGON

10. Great place to make money if you sell rain gear.

9. Fantastic place to start a music career. (Remember the success that Clint Eastwood and Lee Marvin had as singers after *Paint Your Wagon* was filmed here?)

8. "Honey, no sales tax! We can afford Christmas."

7. One of the few locations in the world where the infamous jackalope lives.

6. One of the few places where being a state legislator is a part-time job.

5. The only state in America where the term "Civil War" refers to a game involving beavers, ducks, four quarters and a football.

4. Our 296 miles of beautiful coastline—all publicly owned!

3. Cultural activities that abound in virtually every community ranging from world-class rodeos to Shakespeare, beer tasting and counter-culture country fairs.

2. A professional basketball team that, despite recent setbacks, still makes us proud.

1. Scenic beauty that knows no bounds.

ABOUT THE

Roger Garcia

Roger Garcia emigrated from El Salvador to North America at the age of seven. Because of the language barrier, he had to find a way to communicate with other kids. That's when he discovered the art of tracing and it wasn't long before he mastered this highly skilled technique. He taught himself to paint and sculpt, and then in high school and college, Roger skipped class all day to hide in the art room and further explore his talent. Currently, Roger's work can be seen in a local weekly newspaper.

Patrick Hénaff

Born in France, Patrick Hénaff is a versatile, mostly self-taught artist who has explored a variety of media under many different influences. He now uses primarily pen and ink to draw and then processes the images on computer. He is particularly interested in the narrative power of pictures and tries to use them as a way to tell stories, whether he is working on comic pages, posters, illustrations, cartoons or concept art.

ABOUT THE AUTHORS

Mark Thorburn

Mark Thorburn loves history. He has contributed to and edited several history textbooks and references and has written for newspapers across North America. Mark has lived life as a lawyer, a college instructor and a historian as well as an author. His educational background is broad, with a BA in political science, a law degree from Willamette University and two MA degrees, one in American history from Portland State University. In his free time, Mark plays sports, reads great books, goes to the theater and watches classic films.

Lisa Wojna

Lisa Wojna, author of several other nonfiction books, has worked in the community newspaper industry as a writer and journalist and has traveled all over North America and even to the wilds of Africa. Although writing and photography have been a central part of her life for as long as she can remember, it's the people behind every story that are her motivation and give her the most fulfillment.

www.ingramcontent.com/pod-product-compliance
Lightning Source LLC
Chambersburg PA
CBHW071701090426
42738CB00009B/1617